TOP STORIES 1

ALLAN BAILLIE
ISOBELLE CARMODY
MEREDITH COSTAIN
JACKIE FRENCH
ARCHIMEDE FUSILLO
LIBBY GLEESON
MORRIS GLEITZMAN
ANDY GRIFFITHS
CHRISTINE HARRIS
PAUL JENNINGS
VICTOR KELLEHER
MARGO LANAGAN
SOPHIE MASSON
GARTH NIX
GILLIAN RUBINSTEIN
CAROLE WILKINSON

hi.com.au/topstories

Heinemann
Harcourt Education

Heinemann
HARCOURT EDUCATION
20 Thackray Road, Port Melbourne,
Victoria 3207
hi.com.au
info@hi.com.au

PO Box 460, Port Melbourne, Victoria 3207

Offices in Sydney, Brisbane, Perth and Adelaide. Associated companies, branches and representatives throughout the world.

© This collection, Harcourt Education, a division of Pearson Australia Group Pty Ltd 2007

© Individual stories retained by authors

First published 2007
2010 2009 2008 2007
10 9 8 7 6 5 4 3 2

Reproduction and communication for educational purposes

The Australian *Copyright Act 1968* (the Act) allows a maximum of one chapter or 10% of the pages of this work, whichever is the greater, to be reproduced and/or communicated by any educational institution for its educational purposes provided that that educational institution (or the body that administers it) has given a remuneration notice to Copyright Agency Limited (CAL) under the Act.

For details of the CAL licence for educational institutions contact CAL, Level 15, 233 Castlereagh Street, Sydney, NSW, 2000, tel (02) 9394 7600, fax (02) 9394 7601, email info@copyright.com.au.

Reproduction and communication for other purposes

Except as permitted under the Act (for example any fair dealing for the purposes of study, research, criticism or review), no part of this book may be reproduced, stored in a retrieval system, communicated or transmitted in any form or by any means without prior written permission. All enquiries should be made to the publisher at the address above.

This book is not to be treated as a blackline master; that is, any photocopying beyond fair dealing requires prior written permission.

Publisher: Michael Pryor
Designer: Claire Wilson
Permissions researcher: Gwenda McGough
Coordinating editors: Fiona Maplestone, Steve Dobney

Typeset in 10.5/13 pt Calisto by Claire Wilson

Prepress by Publishing Pre-press, Port Melbourne

Printed and bound by CTPS, China

National Library of Australia cataloguing-in-publication data:

Top stories. 1.
For secondary school students.
ISBN 978 1 74081 838 4

1. Short stories, Australian.

A823.0140809283

Pearson Australia Group Pty Ltd
ABN 40 004 245 943

contents

Bits of an Autobiography I May Not Write ❧ Morris Gleitzman **1**

To Switch or Not To Switch? ❧ Andy Griffiths **11**

Eight Legs, Two Wheels ❧ Carole Wilkinson **19**

Time Flies ❧ Meredith Costain **29**

Missing the Last Laugh ❧ Archimede Fusillo **41**

Doing Time ❧ Christine Harris **49**

Smudge ❧ Jackie French **61**

Haunted ❧ Victor Kelleher **77**

A Dolphin Dream ❧ Gillian Rubinstein **85**

Three Roses ❧ Garth Nix **103**

Round the Bend ❧ Paul Jennings **109**

Snake Man ❧ Sophie Masson **123**

Cheat! ❧ Allan Baillie **131**

Rain ❧ Libby Gleeson **141**

The Red Shoes ❧ Isobelle Carmody **151**

Sweet Pippit ❧ Margo Lanagan **167**

Acknowledgements **187**

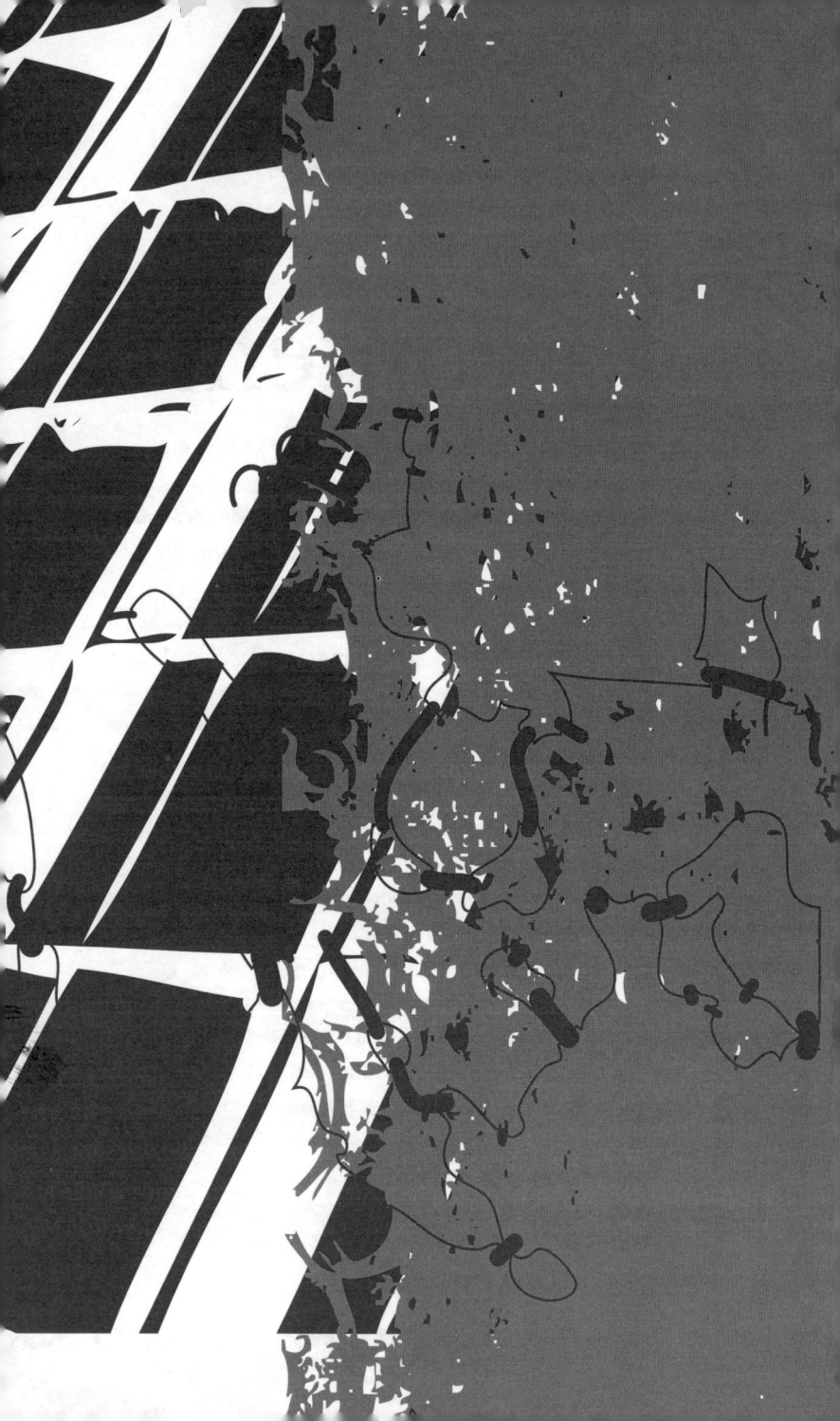

Bits of an Autobiography I May Not Write

Morris Gleitzman

Bits of an Autobiography I May Not Write • Morris Gleitzman

Two weeks of thinking, and still no idea for my next book. I'd tried everything. Meditation. Self-hypnosis. Vacuuming my scalp to stimulate my brain.

Then a letter arrived from a kid in Western Australia. 'Your books are pretty good,' she wrote, 'except for the total lack of motorbikes.'

I fell to my knees, partly in gratitude and partly because the vacuum cleaner was still on my head. At last, a story idea. A kid travelling across the Great Sandy Desert on a motorbike. Not bad.

I'd just finished chapter one when the next letter came.

'Reasonably okay books,' wrote a kid in Adelaide, 'but why so few exotic fish?'

Good point. I rewrote chapter one. It ended up longer, mostly because the bike couldn't travel so fast with the aquarium on the back.

'Your stories would be more interesting,' said a letter from Bristol, 'if they included more elderly people.'

I had to agree. I rewrote chapter one and it certainly was more interesting. Particularly when one of the kid's grandparents, parched from running to keep up with the bike, drank the aquarium and swallowed a coral trout.

It looked like she was a goner until the letter from Philadelphia arrived. 'More sports,' it said. Which is how, in the next draft, the kid came to have a table tennis bat handy to whack Gran on the back.

'Shouldn't you be thinking up your own ideas, Dad?' asked the kids.

'Why?' I replied.

Bits of an Autobiography I May Not Write — Morris Gleitzman

'Oh, no reason,' they shrugged, handing me six letters.

'Waterskiing,' said one. 'Clydesdale horses,' said another. 'Self-reticulating irrigation systems,' said the other four.

This morning when the postman came I hid under my desk. He found me. I was sobbing.

'Must be tough, being a writer,' he said, bending down and handing me a bundle of letters. 'I wouldn't know where to get the ideas from.'

※

It was a proud moment. I'd just built my first piece of furniture and I could feel my chest swelling almost as much as the finger I'd hit with the hammer.

'Well,' I said to the kids, 'what do you think?'

I held my breath as they ran their hands over the four sturdy legs, the finely stitched upholstery and the skilfully-hung mirrored door.

'Funny-looking bookshelves, Dad,' they said. My chest deflated. They were right. Who was I trying to kid? I was a writer, not a handyman.

'Do-It-Yourself furniture,' I said bitterly. 'If there's anyone who can build this stuff themselves I'd like to know their secret.'

The kids looked at the empty boxes strewn around the room. 'Perhaps,' they said gently, 'it involves assembling the bookcase, the settee, the coffee table and the bathroom cabinet as four separate items.'

'It was the instructions,' I said. 'They were impossible to understand. Look at that diagram. I broke three screwdrivers trying to follow that.'

The kids sighed. 'It's the furniture shop logo,' they said.

I realised my problem was that I didn't speak the language of Do-It-Yourself. I started at language school the following week.

Bits of an Autobiography I May Not Write • Morris Gleitzman

The other students were doing French, Spanish and Japanese. I enrolled in Furniture Assembly.

The instructor tried hard, but by the ninth week I still couldn't translate 'slot base support bracket A into side panel rib B'. I couldn't even say it.

'I'm sorry,' said the instructor. 'I can't do any more for you.'

I looked at him pleadingly. 'Not even put my bookshelves together?'

He shook his head.

At home, I stared gloomily at the bookshelf assembly instructions. Why could I construct a story but not a piece of furniture? Then I noticed the instructions were looking different. They were in the kids' handwriting. 'One fine day,' I read excitedly, 'a base support bracket named A met a side panel rib called B ...'

Drop in and see my new bookshelves some time. They look great.

❧

The kids stared at the peanut butter, beetroot, sardine and pineapple sandwich.

'Dad,' they pleaded, 'couldn't you make it plain old cheese and tomato?'

I put the sandwich into the lunchbox and explained that I'd decided to make something special for the first day.

'But this isn't our first day,' said the kids. 'We've been going to school for years.'

I added a kiwi fruit, two gherkins and some kangaroo salami to the lunchbox. 'It's my new book's first day,' I said, voice trembling. 'At the publishers'.'

The kids stared at the manuscript. They stared at the woolly scarf tied round it and the knitted hat pulled down snugly over

Bits of an Autobiography I May Not Write ❧ Morris Gleitzman

the title page. Then they stared at me. 'You're making your new book a packed lunch?' they croaked.

'Please,' I said. 'It isn't easy, saying goodbye to a manuscript. Sending it off to that big scary building. It's almost as upsetting as your first day at school, and you remember how upsetting that was.'

The kids said they did, particularly the sandwiches.

My eyes misted over. 'It's only a 96-page kids' book,' I sobbed as I filled its plastic drink bottle. 'What if it gets bullied by a 600-page truck repair manual?'

The kids took me to one side. 'Dad,' they said quietly, 'remember how you were a bit over-protective when we started school? Getting your helicopter licence and joining the traffic police so you could hover over the playground at lunchtime?'

I pulled myself together. 'It's okay,' I said. 'I'm not going to embarrass my new book like that.'

And I meant it. Which is why I got the job as the window-cleaner. Far less noticeable and I was still able to keep an eye on my baby from the extension ladder.

That's how I was the first to know about the tragedy. The publishers decided to delay publication of my new manuscript. First they made me write them a sandwich recipe book.

❧

The judge looked sternly down at me. 'You have been charged,' he said, 'with one of the most serious crimes ever to be tried in this courtroom. How do you plead?'

The public gallery was packed and the jury was staring at me accusingly. My mouth felt like a sandpit in the Simpson Desert.

'Not guilty,' I croaked. 'I'm innocent. I didn't do it. Honest.'

The prosecutor was on her feet. 'I put it to you,' she said, 'that on 14th of April last, at bedtime, you read your children *The Twits* by Roald Dahl and that you wilfully and intentionally left out the bit about the wormy spaghetti because you didn't want to miss the start of the wrestling on telly.'

'Not true,' I cried. 'It wasn't wrestling, it was showjumping.'

The public gallery gasped. The jury narrowed their eyes. I put my head in my hands.

'All right,' I sobbed, 'I admit it. I couldn't bear to read it all again. I'd read it 127 times in the past year alone.'

My kids took the witness stand. 'That wasn't the worst example,' they said. 'In May he read us *War and Peace* and all we got was, "Once upon a time there was a war, and then there was peace, the end."'

'I couldn't stand it again,' I sobbed. 'Not for the eleventh time.'

'And that,' said the prosecutor, 'was the same week he read you "Ode to a Nightingale"?'

The kids looked at me sadly. 'He said it was Keats,' they murmured, 'but we just didn't think that "Tweet, tweet, okay kids, time to settle down now, *The Bill*'s started" sounded much like a classic poem.'

It was a long trial. I was found guilty. I anxiously studied the judge's wig, hoping to see the telltale sticky fingermarks that would reveal he understood what it was to be a parent. There weren't any. So when he read out my jail sentence he didn't skip a single bit. But then, he was only eleven.

᠅

'Dad,' said the kids, 'why are you kneeling on the floor with your head in the fridge? Have you got a headache?'

I explained I hadn't, I was just telling the tops of the plastic salad containers about my schooldays.

The kids both stared at me.

'It's one of my New Year resolutions,' I explained, showing them the list I'd made. 'See? Number four.'

Bits of an Autobiography I May Not Write • Morris Gleitzman

'*Spend more time talking to the kids,*' read the ten-year-old.

I took the list back. 'Does it say kids?' I said, squinting at it. 'I could have sworn it said lids.'

The kids sighed. So did the lids.

'Pity you haven't kept the first New Year resolution on your list,' said the kids.

'I have,' I said, squeaking to my feet and showing them my bright yellow rubber footwear. 'See? *Get new galoshes.*'

The kids sighed again. 'Dad,' they groaned, pointing to the list, 'It says *get new glasses.*'

'Oh dear,' I said, squinting again at the blurry writing. A chill crept up my spine and not just because I'd left the fridge door open. 'Um,' I said, 'I'm feeling a bit bad now about New Year resolutions two and three.'

The kids studied the list. '*Two,*' they read, '*polish the car.* What's wrong with that?'

I took them outside and pointed up to the roof. 'There's no car up there,' said the kids. Then they saw the shiny cat.

The cat slid off the roof, leaving a trail of Supa-Shine wax on the tiles. The kids caught it, glared at me and we went inside.

'Number three can't be worse than that,' they said. I could feel a headache coming on, so I put my head in the fridge.

The kids read out number three. '*Get more sleep.* What's so bad about that?'

I closed my eyes, laid my head down next to the lettuce and waited for them to hear the baa-ing coming from the living room.

It had been a hard day and now, as I slumped wearily down at the dinner table, the kids were staring at me.

Bits of an Autobiography I May Not Write • Morris Gleitzman

'What's the matter?' I said. 'Haven't you ever seen a bloke with oil on his hands and grease in his armpits and soot on his face and electrical burns on his scalp?'

'Not one that says he's a children's author,' they replied accusingly. 'You've been fibbing to us, haven't you, Dad? You don't write kids' books at all, you lubricate heavy mining equipment.'

I sighed and took them into my study. 'The days are gone,' I said, 'when all you needed to write a book was a pencil and six rolls of toilet paper. It's a high-tech business these days, being an author. And some days you trip over the computer cable and slosh coffee into the printer and the explosion sends you reeling back into the photocopier, which short-circuits the fax machine and melts the modem.'

The kids looked at the smoking wreckage. 'What you need,' they said, 'is to get back in touch with the simple things in life. Why don't you take up gardening?'

My motto is try anything once unless it gives you dandruff, so the next morning I put on an old jumper and went out the back to grow things.

The kids appeared a couple of hours later. 'Dad,' they yelled. 'What are you doing?'

I paused to wipe the sump oil out of my ears. 'Planting carrots,' I said. 'But first I have to clear these weeds.'

I realise now it was taking my hand off the chainsaw that allowed it to rear up and knock the flame-thrower against the handbrake of the bulldozer.

I'm in hospital now and it's great. I've been on the X-ray machine and the ultrasound machine and the electro-cardiogram machine, and tomorrow they're putting me on the brain-scan machine. I'm looking forward to that. Just as long as the doctor doesn't spill his coffee.

TO SWITCH OR NOT TO SWITCH?

Andy Griffiths

To Switch or Not To Switch? ⁂ Andy Griffiths

LIFE is full of challenges. Even a seemingly simple act, such as choosing which lane to stand in at the supermarket, can be fraught with difficulties. For instance, consider the following situation:

You are in a supermarket, and you have nine items in your basket. One of the items is a packet of condoms. It is the only item you really want—you only put the others in the basket to disguise the fact that you are buying condoms. Not that there's anything wrong with buying condoms—they make great heavy-duty water-bombs—but it's possible that people might mistakenly think you want them for something else.

DILEMMA #1: *You are about to take your place in the express lane, but then you notice that it is only for shoppers with eight items or less. Should you try to sneak through and hope that nobody is counting, or should you go and join the regular queue?*

It's a tough decision. One item over the eight-item limit is hardly going to make a big difference to the speed at which you pass through the checkout. And yet the lane is clearly marked '8 items or less'. Can you be arrested for trying to smuggle more than the allowable number of items through an express lane? Of course not. You decide to go for it. But then you look at the other people in the lane. They are all doing the right thing. They all have eight items or less in their baskets. It's not really very fair to them. And deep down you are not a bad person. You decide to go through a regular checkout.

DILEMMA #2: *Is it better to stand behind one person w[ith a] trolley stuffed full of items, or to stand in a queue of three [people] who only have a small basket of items each?*

To Switch or Not To Switch? — Andy Griffiths

This is like one of those trick questions in a maths test. You want to pick the obvious answer, but you know that the obvious answer will be wrong, so you pick the other one. Which turns out to be wrong, because that's just what the person who wrote the test wanted you to do. Give up! It doesn't mater which queue you pick. The other queue will always move faster. It's the law of supermarket queues. So, after a quick game of eenie-meenie-minie-moh, you take your place behind the person with the full trolley.

DILEMMA #3: *Nothing happens. The other queue is moving, but not yours. Or are you just imagining it? Is it just one of those 'the grass is always greener on the other side of the fence' situations? Do you stick with your original hunch and stay in the lane you're in or do you cut your losses and change queues? To switch or not to switch?—that is the question.*

You're watching the people in the other checkout. They're practically sprinting—just hurling their stuff and their money at the cashier—who in turn is just throwing them the bags and their change as they're running out the door. Meanwhile you're stuck in the same spot reading and rereading the headlines on the latest *Woman's Day*: Royal blah this ... royal blah that ... You can't stand it any more. You don't give a royal raspberry about the royals. All you want is to be outside in the sun chucking water-bombs at your friends. You switch lanes.

And then it becomes clear. The old guy doesn't actually *want* a Bavarian cheese cake. He's only buying it to annoy *you*. He's the same old guy who is always shuffling in front of you in the mall. The same old guy who always manages to get to the ATM just before you do ... It's hard to believe, but this old guy has nothing better to do than to devote his entire life to driving you insane.

DILEMMA #5: *Should you give in to the powerful urge to grab the back of the old guy's head and push his face repeatedly into the Bavarian cheese cake while screaming 'Next time get one with the price on it Grandpa!' ... or should you resist this impulse in case it attracts attention to you and your condoms?*

You take a deep breath. You count to ten. You resist. You take another deep breath ... and just when you're feeling calm, you notice that there is a sign hanging from the register 'CASHIER IN TRAINING'.

DILEMMA #6: *You know you should switch aisles immediately because these cashiers-in-training are the slowest of all possible cashiers—but you're worried that if they see you leave it might hurt their feelings. They might break down and start crying. And the supermarket manager will come over and ask: 'Who upset this cashier?' and everybody in the entire supermarket will turn around and point to you, and they'll say in unison, 'That person there! The one with the condoms in the shopping basket!'*

So you don't switch. Everybody's got to learn some time. You hang in there, giving little encouraging smiles to the nervous cashier, trying not to let them see how close you are to breaking open the packet of condoms and going berserk with water-bombs. *Royal blah this ... Royal blah that ... aaagghhhh!*

DILEMMA #7: *They announce that they're opening the lane next to the one you're in. You think, yes! It's the perfect excuse I need to get* *away from the cashier-in-training. But the woman in front of you has been there longer. Should you give her the chance to move there first?*

You don't want to appear really selfish by dashing across and cutting her out, so you pause for a moment to give her the option. But she doesn't move—probably too busy reading about the royals—and in the meantime five other people dash over and you've lost your chance. And now the old guy with the Bavarian cheese cake has forgotten his PIN number. By the time he's punched every possible configuration of numbers on the key-pad the five people in the recently opened aisle are through and you're only just unloading your basket onto the conveyor belt.

DILEMMA #8: *It's your turn. The cashier smiles and says 'Hello, how are you?' You pause. Is it a good idea to say, 'Well, not too bad considering that I've just spent the last three and a half thousand years stuck in a queue thanks to the fact that you are the crappiest cashier-in-training in whose lane I've ever had the misfortune to be stuck,' or should you just keep quiet and not antagonise them in any way in case they retaliate by calling for a price check on your condoms just to embarrass you in front of the whole supermarket?*

You decide to play it safe. You smile. You're very polite. You're doing really well, too, until the cashier says, 'Is this all you've got? You should have gone through the express lane'.

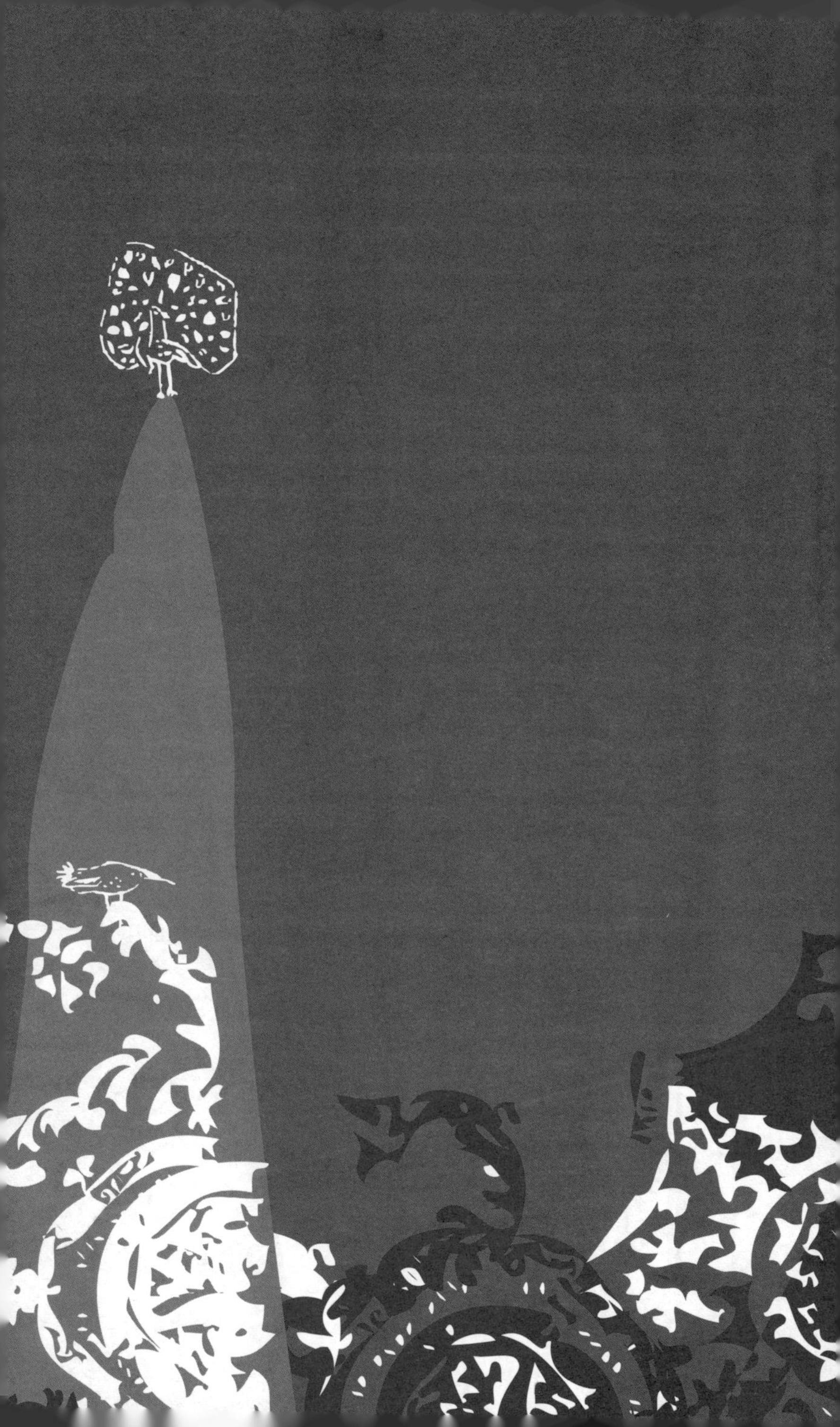

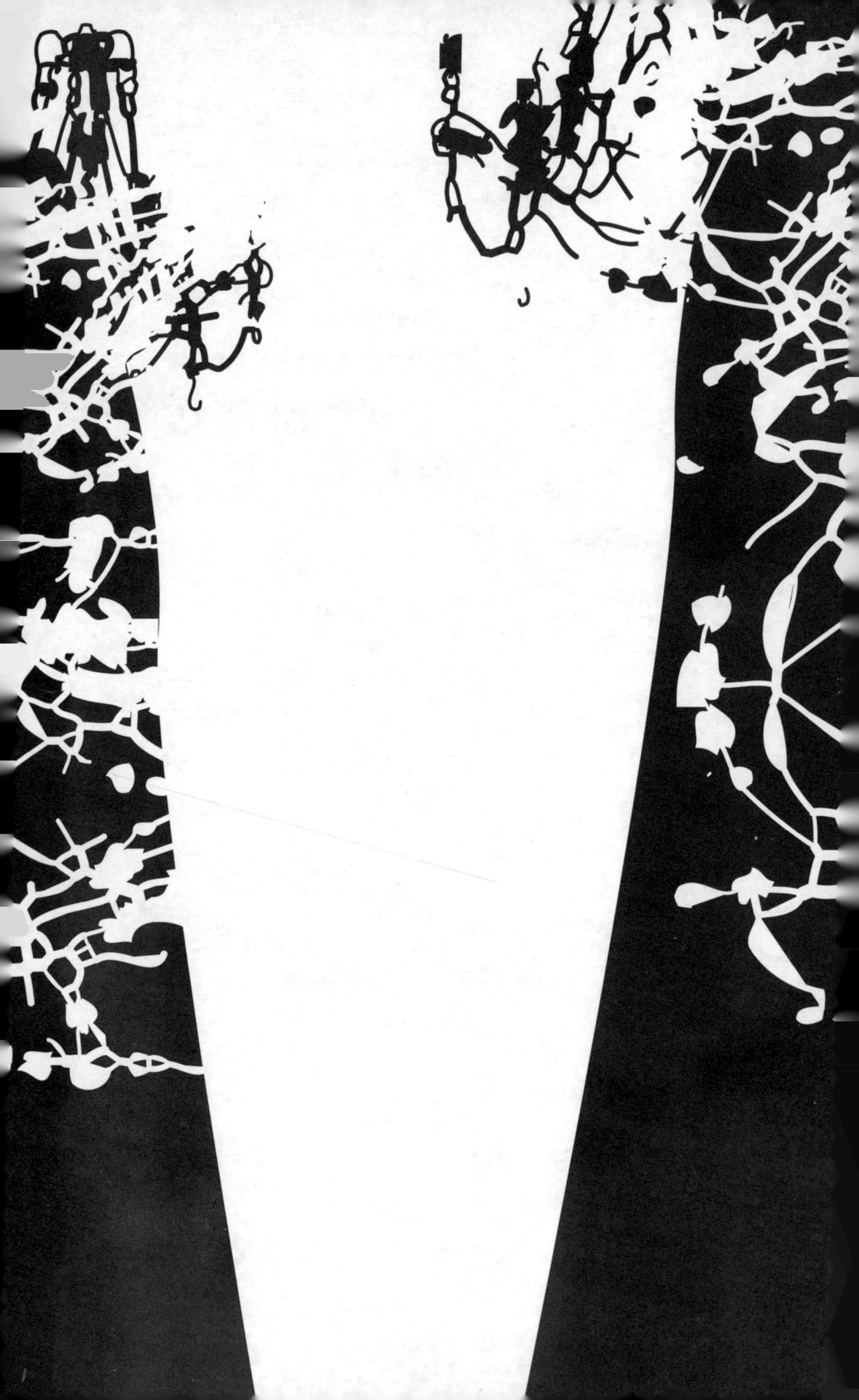

Eight Legs, Two Wheels

Carole Wilkinson

Eight Legs, Two Wheels • Carole Wilkinson

'How do you feel about spiders?'

The man at the bike shop gave the handlebars a final polish. 'There's one that lives on this bike somewhere.' He chuckled as he adjusted the seat. 'Great big huntsman the size of a saucer. I call him Alvin.'

'I don't mind spiders,' I said casually.

I lied. I'm petrified of spiders. Not only the big ones, but the little ones too. Even the ones that are so small you can hardly tell whether they're a spider or an ant. I hate them. I gave the man his money (35 ten-dollar notes) and wheeled my new bike out of the shop. He was still chuckling. He's having me on, I thought. He's the sort of grown-up who likes giving kids a hard time.

All the same it wasn't a very comfortable ride home. I kept imagining I could feel hairy legs climbing up inside my shorts. I stopped six times to check. When I got home I went over the bike from front to back. There just aren't that many places a big spider can hide. I took the seat off and examined every square millimetre. No sign of a spider of any size. I could relax. It was a joke.

It's a fantastic bike. Not brand-new, but it's got everything I'd ever wanted—21-speed gears, dual suspension forks, alloy wheels. It's got a cycle computer as well, so I can tell how far I've travelled and how fast. There's nothing flash on it—no pink lightning bolt transfers, no ribbons or air horns. It's a bike for serious bike riding.

It took me two years to save up for it. I'm too young to get an after-school job in a supermarket, but I delivered junk mail, walked dogs and mowed lawns. I saved my train fare and walked to school. I didn't spend a cent of my pocket money in all that time.

I rode my bike to school the following Monday morning and it felt fine. The little kids gathered around to admire it when I put it in the bike rack. I was proud. Then I saw Kylie Trout.

Did I mention Kylie before? Probably not. I try to forget she exists. She's made my life miserable since I was five years old. Kylie Primrose Chandra Trout. With a name like that, you'd think she'd be the one having a hard time. You might also think I'd be embarrassed about being scared of a girl. You haven't seen Kylie. She's two years older than me. She's thirteen and in high school.

That's where she should have been on that Monday morning, but she wags school a lot and one of her favourite pastimes is going back to her old primary school. Some kids go back to their old school to tell the teachers how they're doing or to give talks to kids just about to go to high school. Kylie comes back to block the toilets or put soapsuds in the frog pond.

All the little kids ran when they saw Kylie leaning over the fence. I wanted to run too, but I had to lock up my bike. I'd bought the strongest D-lock available, with a combination lock rather than a key.

'Nice bike, Ratface,' she said.

'Thanks,' I said. Pathetic, I know, but what else do you say to a girl who lifts bags of cement for a hobby? She's got muscles like you've never seen. It looks like she's got potatoes shoved up her sleeves.

'A person could use a bike like that,' she said.

You'll never get your hands on it, Kylie Trout, I said to myself. It's easy to be tough when the assembly teacher is ringing the bell, less than thirty metres away.

Eight Legs, Two Wheels • Carole Wilkinson

When I came out into the yard at recess time, the little kids came rushing over.

'Come and look at your bike, Michael,' they said. I went into a cold sweat. Kylie. What had she done?

It was right where I'd left it and still locked to the bike rack. It wasn't damaged, but there was something wrong. It was upside down and locked by the back wheel. I don't know how she did it, but it was a warning. She was letting me know that she was still after me.

I lay in bed that night carefully scanning the bedroom ceiling with a torch. I always have to check that there are none of those daddy-long-legs spiders lurking in corners.

I know what they're up to. They're waiting. As soon as I turn the light off they'll dangle down on a thread and crawl all over me. I used to get Mum to come and get them, but she'd catch them in a jar and take them out to the garden. What's the point of that? They'll just walk right back inside again.

Now I knock them down with a broom and splat them with a boot. It's scary. What if I miss and they jump on me? But it's the best way. The only good spider is one that's squashed flat. There were no daddy-long-legs that night, so I stopped worrying about spiders and started worrying about Kylie.

Don't ask me why she picked me as her number one victim all those years ago. I mean, I was five years old, fresh out of kindergarten. I still wore those plastic see-through sandals. I had teddy-bear pyjamas. What sort of seven-year-old picks on a kid on their first ever day at school? Kylie Trout, that's who.

She ate my lunch, spilt my drink and stood on my finger painting. That was just the beginning. Mean? You've never seen mean until you've seen Kylie in a bad mood. And I've never seen her in any other sort of mood. I thought about leaving my bike at home and catching the train. But how dumb is that? No, I'd just have to be careful.

Eight Legs, Two Wheels • Carole Wilkinson

The next weekend the whole family went out for a ride along the river. Mum and Dad on their rusty old bikes, Nicola in a bike seat singing 'The Wheels on the Bike Go Round and Round'.

A family bike ride wasn't quite what I had in mind though. I wanted to go on a long ride all by myself. I mean seriously long, like to Alice Springs or the Gold Coast. I know, they'd never let an eleven-year-old do that. An all day ride along the bike path would have to do, right out to the country and back. It took me three weeks to convince my parents, but in the end I wore them down.

I set out at 9 am. It was perfect weather—the sun was shining but it wasn't too hot. Mum gave me sandwiches. Dad told me not to speed. Nicola cried and wanted to go too. I put on my helmet, set my cycle computer and waved goodbye. I was free. I passed all the other suckers with their parents telling them to slow down and wait for their little brothers, all the losers doing their pathetic tricks on their purple BMXs. I was the king of the bike path.

I rode out past the children's farm, past the rapids where the Olympic kayakers practise. I stopped to admire the view where the river bends back on itself. I was leaning on the handlebars, and happened to glance down.

Eight eyes were staring at me. Eight stripy legs were wrapped around my bell. Two great fangs were practically touching my nose. It was the biggest spider I've ever seen. I jumped a mile. My bike was about to fall over when a hand reached out and caught it. Kylie Trout's.

'You should be more careful,' she said. 'You wouldn't want to scratch your nice new bike.'

'Leave my bike alone!' I yelled.

That was my first mistake. You never yell at Kylie.

'Okay,' she said.

Eight Legs, Two Wheels • Carole Wilkinson

She let go of my bike and it crashed onto the path. I winced at the thought of all my gears buckling.

I went to pick it up. Kylie grabbed it first. 'It's not a bad bike. Probably worth a bit.'

'You can't have it, it's mine.'

'And who's going to stop me?'

'Alvin,' I said. I was thinking so fast I surprised myself.

'Who's Alvin?'

'My pet spider. He's as big as a saucer and he lives on my bike.' I glanced at the bike. There was no sign of the spider.

'Oh yeah. Pull the other one, Ratface.'

She started wheeling my precious bike away.

'I'll tell the police.'

That was my second mistake. Threatening Kylie is like giving her an invitation to do something worse.

'You do and I'll break your arm.'

I believed her. She'd broken plenty of bones on the hockey field. A cyclist in Lycra bike shorts rode by.

'Help!' I yelled. 'That girl's stealing my bike.'

That was my third mistake. If you tell on Kylie she goes crazy. The cyclist was listening to a Walkman. He didn't even hear me.

'That does it,' said Kylie. She swung an enormous thigh over my bike, and parked her huge bottom on the seat. 'From now on this is my bike.'

She rode off. I ran after her but she was going really fast. Then I heard a scream and she suddenly veered off the bike path and into a barrier. Kylie and the bike parted company. My bike crashed to the ground. Kylie went over the handlebars and into the river. It was a beautiful sight.

Eight Legs, Two Wheels • Carole Wilkinson

I rushed up to my bike. I just caught sight of eight hairy legs tucking themselves in under the front mudguard. So that's where the spider lived!

'I see you met Alvin,' I said to Kylie as she dragged herself onto the bank.

I didn't make it to the country. I spent the rest of the day at the bike shop getting the front wheel straightened.

'Have you met Alvin yet?' asked the bike shop owner.

'Yep,' I said. 'We're good friends.'

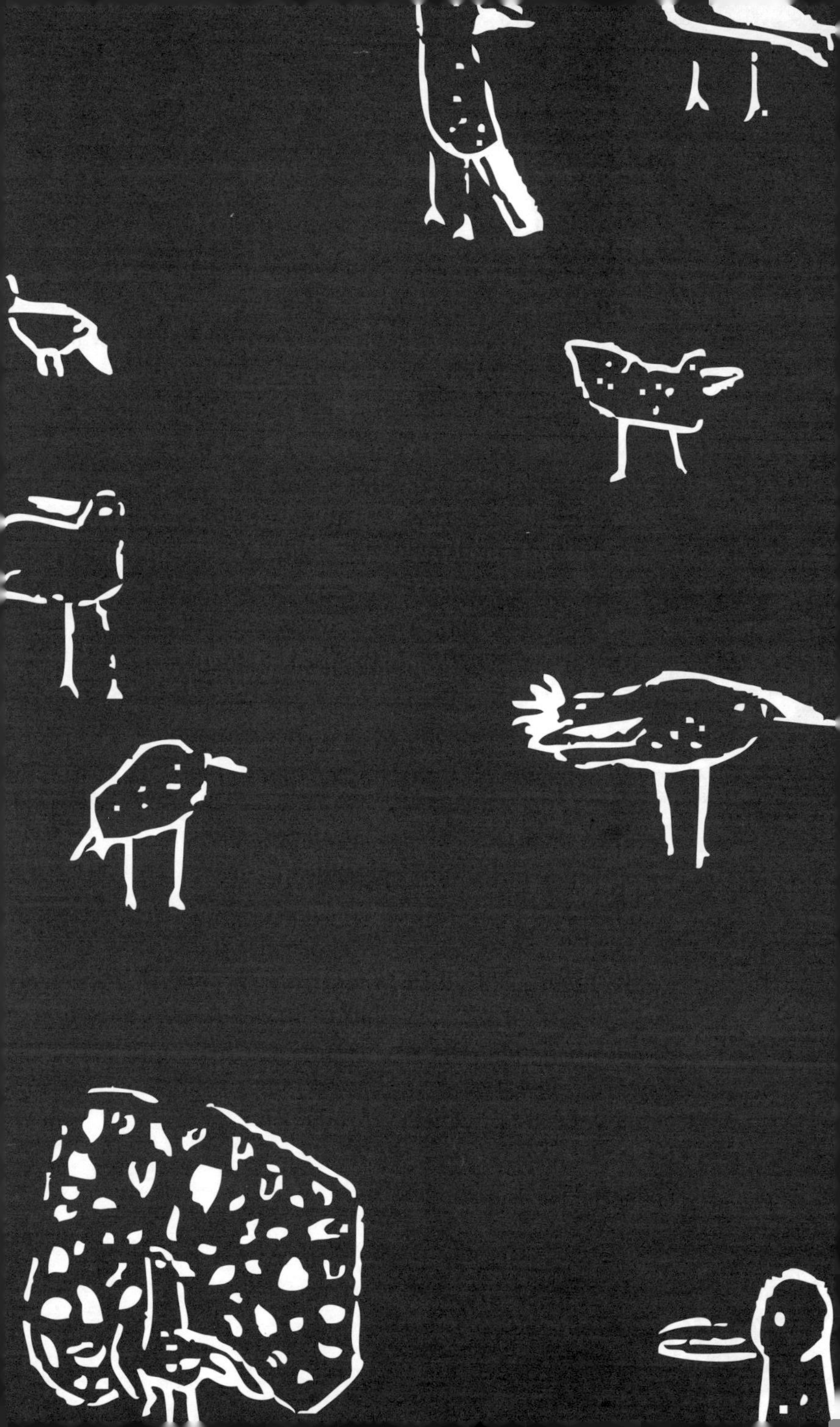

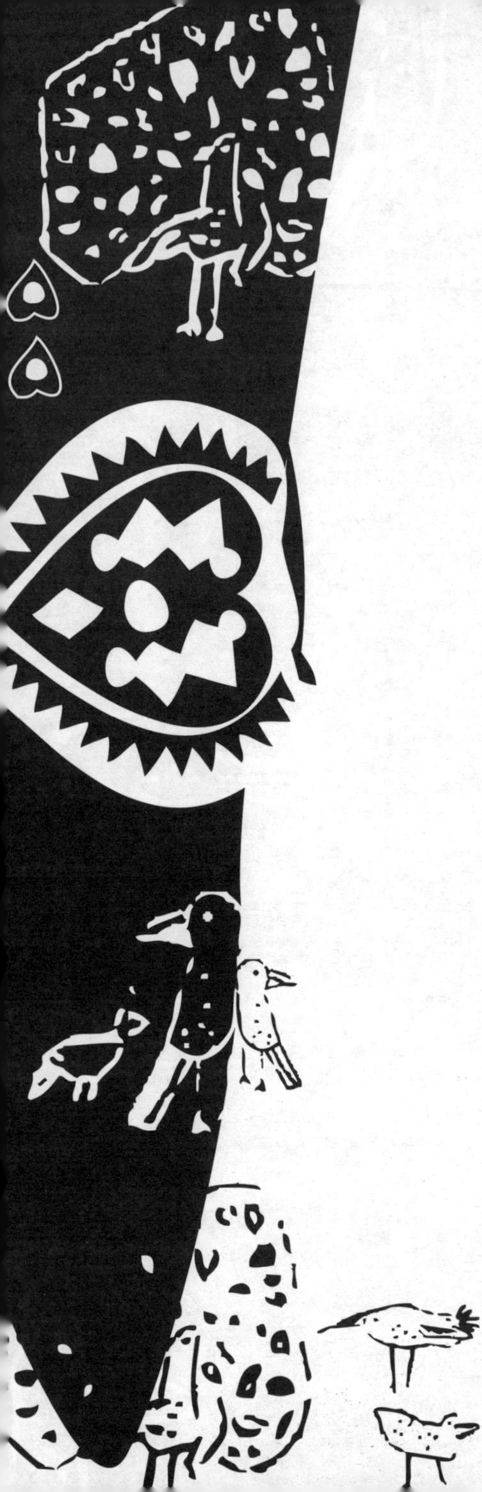

TIME FLIES

Meredith Costain

Time Flies • Meredith Costain

BEN TEMPLETON had only one thought on his mind. Lunch. A nice, cool cafe; somewhere where he could sit down, have a burger and shake, and stop tramping round the city looking at 'culture'.

He fiddled with his baseball cap for a bit, then sneaked a look at his watch: 11.25. Not long to go now. His grandparents had been whipping him in and out of art galleries and up and down the steps of public buildings all morning.

'Come along, Ben,' said his grandmother. 'Stop dawdling. We've just got time to go up the clock tower and have a look at the city before we stop for a nice bite of lunch. Haven't we, Ron?'

'S'right, love,' said his grandfather. 'This way, son.' He steered Ben towards the City Square.

The clock tower? Ben gulped. It must be over two hundred metres tall! They weren't expecting him to walk up stairs for two hundred metres, were they? Not after all that shoe leather he'd put in this morning, trudging round looking at paintings of skinny men and fat women. Some of them hadn't had many clothes on! It had been embarrassing.

But when they got to the clock tower, he was saved after all. There was a lift.

There was also a small queue of people, waiting to go up the tower. The clock tower was a popular tourist attraction in the city. The view from the top was spectacular. Well, so his grandfather said anyway. Ben wasn't so sure. The streets he'd walked through that morning had seemed fairly ordinary, much like the ones in his own city. He'd told his grandfather that. But he'd just smiled at him, in a knowing way.

'You'll see, son,' he'd said. 'You'll see.'

Ben's stomach rumbled. Everything was so boring. His grandparents especially. They were always yabbering on about something. Do this. Look at that. They never shut up.

His grandfather was yabbering away at him now. Something about the plaque that was hanging above the entrance to the lift. There were two words engraved on it, in scrawly writing:

Tempus Fugit

'Tempus fuggit,' said Ben, reading the words for something to do. 'What's that mean?'

'It's fyoo-jit. Tempus fyoojit,' corrected his grandfather. 'It's Latin. Don't they teach you anything at school these days?'

Nothing you'd like, thought Ben. His stomach rumbled again. They were always going on about how thin he was. You'd think they'd want to make a point of feeding him! Often. Oh, why wasn't it lunchtime yet? He checked his watch: 11.33.

'Time flies,' said his grandfather.

Only when you're having fun, thought Ben, which he definitely wasn't. How could he, stuck around boring adults all day long? Hadn't they ever been kids themselves? Then again, maybe they hadn't. He tried to imagine his grandmother mucking around and gave up. Fat chance!

'Huh?' he said out loud.

'Tempus fugit,' repeated his grandfather, shaking his head. 'Time flies. That's what it means, son.'

'It's because of the clock tower, see,' explained his grandmother. 'It's a little joke about the clock.'

Some joke, thought Ben. There was a jarring, rasping sound, and the lift, carrying a full load of Japanese tourists, whooshed down towards them.

The doors slowly opened and the cage disgorged its passengers. Another group filed in and the doors soundlessly closed again. Ben just had time to glimpse pink padded walls and a man wearing a peaked cap and a navy jacket standing at the controls before the lift whooshed off again, out of sight.

Tempus fugit, tempus fugit, he repeated over and over to himself, as his grandmother droned on about the paintings in the gallery they'd just visited. Why were old people always so boring?

Ben put his ear to the wall. He could hear the hum of the cables as the lift strained upwards. He thought of the man in the peaked cap he'd seen, driving the lift. What a loser! Going up and down in a lift all day. He wouldn't get to see much either—just the top and the bottom of the building. And tourists. People like his grandparents, who yabbered on all day about what they'd seen, and what they were going to see next. Awful.

He put his watch to his ear and listened to the faint ticking. Tempus fugit. Tempus fugit. Come on, time. Fly. Get me out of here. Fast.

The cables hummed and the doors slid open again. 'Mind your step,' said the liftman in a dull voice to no one in particular. Like he'd said it every day—year in, year out. 'Mind your step.'

And then his grandfather was pushing him in the small of his back and guiding him into the lift. They were the last in the queue. Ben was squashed between a fat lady on his left and thick, upholstered padding on the lift wall on his right.

The doors clanked shut. Inside the lift it was hot and airless. Ben couldn't see much around the sides of the fat lady, but he could feel the thick carpeting under his feet, and smell the velvety plush of the padded walls. It was like being inside a giant coffin. Only it was worse. The liftman talked to them all the way up to the top of the tower.

'Ahem. The history of the clock tower,' he recited tonelessly. His voice was hollow and dry. 'The City Hall Clock Tower was built in 1865. Designed by Mr Ernest Harridan, a member of the British Horological society, the tower rises one hundred and

Time Flies • Meredith Costain

ninety-six metres above the ground. There are four clock faces, each five metres in diameter, with minute hands that are three metres long.'

'Have any of the clocks ever stopped?' asked his grandfather, grinning around at the other tourists.

But the lift-driver ignored him, ploughing relentlessly on.

'The chimes ring every hour, on the hour. The chimes consist of an hour bell, weighing 4.56 tonnes ...'

'Goodness,' said his grandmother. 'Imagine all that metal up there! How ever did they get it up to the top?'

'... weighing 4.56 tonnes,' repeated the liftman, in his stride now, determined not to be interrupted, 'and four smaller bells, each weighing slightly over three tonnes.'

'Testy old coot, isn't he?' remarked Ben's grandfather to the old man standing next to him. 'You'd think he'd be happy to answer our questions.'

'Ooh, he's a devil,' wheezed the old man. 'I've been going up in this lift to see the city since I was a boy. Now I bring my grandchildren—and *their* children,' he added, patting a ginger-haired boy on the head, 'and he hasn't changed in all that time. Natter, natter, natter. Talk, talk, talk. I've never known him to be interrupted. Not once!'

Huh? Thought Ben. This old guy had been coming here all those years and had always had the *same* lift-driver? By the look of him—baggy pants and silvery whiskers—he'd have to be pushing ninety! He must be mixing up all the lift-drivers he'd seen in his time.

The liftman glared at his charges, as though they were naughty schoolkids not paying attention. 'The first blow of the chimes is heard exactly on the hour,' he said loudly.

Ben's grandfather jumped in, determined not to be put down. 'On the hour, you say. That's quite soon, isn't it! Will we hear the chimes as we go past?'

The lift-driver's face turned an angry shade of red. He paused, then turned to face Ben's grandfather with the look of a snake about to strike. 'I don't take the lift up while the clock's chiming,' he said softly. 'It's more than the human ear can stand.' As he swivelled back to face the controls, Ben caught his eye. It was cold and hard. Ice-blue. He shivered slightly, even though it was uncomfortably hot in the lift.

The lift reached the top, but the doors remained closed. The lift-driver looked around the compartment, making sure he had everyone's attention before he spoke again.

'There are stairs to the observation platform. The lift can only go so far. Narrow stairs,' he hissed, looking meaningfully at the fat lady, who gasped indignantly. 'Mind how you go.' He pushed a button and the doors slid open.

Jammed against the wall, Ben was the last to leave the lift. He shot a look at the lift-driver. Talk about rude! That lady probably couldn't help being fat. The lift-driver stared back at him, his eyes vacant, but somehow seeming to hold Ben's. He shivered again, and, pushing past the people slowly making their way up the twisting staircase, bounded up to the observation platform.

Walking round to the back of the tower, away from the camera-snapping tourists, Ben felt as though he had entered another world. It was a fine, clear day, and the sun blazed down, bouncing off glass-sided buildings and lighting up the city spread out before him like a relief map. Birds wheeled in the sky, chasing each other around the rooftops. The traffic noise was muted, dull. He could see tiny people wandering the city footpaths, carrying briefcases and shopping bags, heading off to meetings and other boring things adults did in their free time.

Ben had never been up this high before. He felt slightly light-headed, yet curiously powerful. Powerful and free, just like the birds soaring around the chiselled stonework. Yet his thoughts

Time Flies • Meredith Costain

kept returning to the man driving the lift. He wondered if he ever left his post to come up and admire the view, or whether he toiled relentlessly on, repeating his spiel about the history of the clock tower time and time again to lift-loads of tourists.

'Great view, eh, son?'

His grandfather was at his shoulder, pointing out in a booming voice the city landmarks—Parliament House, the Treasury, the river snaking through the high-rise buildings.

'We'd better go down now if we want to get to the Planetarium on time,' interrupted his grandmother.

They filed slowly down the stairs, Ben dragging his feet. He'd actually liked it up there, on top of the world; didn't want to leave. The lift-driver was waiting for them, looking meaningfully this time at his watch, ushering them into the plush compartment where the rest of the tourists stood waiting.

Ben closed his eyes as the lift plummeted downwards, leaving his stomach behind somewhere on the rooftop. He opened them again to see the lift-driver watching him, a mocking glint in his own ice-blue ones. 'Ground floor,' intoned the liftman. 'Mind your step.'

The doors slid open and the people streamed out, heading off for drinks, for lunch, for more sightseeing. Ben's grandmother consulted her watch. 'Five minutes to twelve. We'll just get a picture of you, Ben dear, on the City Hall steps, before we go off for lunch.'

But when she looked through her handbag, she realised her camera was missing. 'Gone!' she squawked. 'Nicked!'

'Now calm down, love.' Ben's grandfather clucked and fussed around her. 'Where did you see it last?'

She pointed to the top of the clock tower, glinting in the midday sun. 'Up there. I took that picture of you leaning against the parapet. And then I put it down for a minute while you showed me where the car was parked.'

'Then that's where it still is, silly,' said Ben's grandfather. 'Up you go, son, and fetch it down. Those long legs of yours are much fitter than ours.'

Ben looked up at the main clockface. Both the minute and hour hands were hovering dangerously close to the twelve. 'But ...' he began. The lift-driver had said he wouldn't take people up the tower while the clock was striking.

'No buts, son. Just do it. Off you go, before one of those birds knocks it down and smashes it.'

Ben shuffled towards the lift, his feet leaden. Part of him wanted to go up again to the top of the tower, to that curious sense of freedom at the top of the world. And the other part hung back with dread. Dread of getting back into the lift again, that padded coffin, with the man with the creepy eyes. *Alone*.

Stalling for time, he looked at his watch again, then back at his grandparents. Go on, they nodded and smiled. The words on the plaque above the lift door glared down at him. *Tempus fugit*. Time flies. The lift-driver stood there waiting, his hand lightly brushing the controls, the mocking look in his eyes again. Or was he just imagining it? Maybe the man was just bored, anxious to get off for his own well-deserved lunch break.

Ben stepped into the lift. The doors clicked smoothly shut behind him. He felt his stomach waver again as the lift slowly rose, heard the clank and hum of the cables. Without the other people in the lift the carpet looked thicker, the plush-padded walls more suffocating. The lift clanked slowly, inexorably, upwards.

As soon as it reached the top, Ben clambered out, raced up the narrow stairs to the part of the balcony where his grandparents had been. He spotted the camera immediately.

Once again, he was struck by the other-worldly feeling at the top of the tower. He peered down over the edge to the City Square, where his grandparents stood, waiting. He gave them a

Time Flies • Meredith Costain

little wave, holding up the camera to show them he'd found it. Then it was down the stairs again to the lift.

At the doors, he hesitated. Surely the driver wouldn't operate the lift this close to twelve o'clock! Not when the bells were about to chime. The eyes of the liftman caught and held his. He felt himself being pulled towards the lift and in through the open door. *Ssssshhhttt*. The doors slid shut.

The silence in the lift was stultifying. Ben could hear his own tiny watch ticking. The lift-driver turned to face him. 'Ahem,' he said as he cleared his throat. 'The history of the clock tower …'

'There's no need,' said Ben nervously. 'I heard it before, th… the first time.'

'The City Hall Clock Tower was built in 1865,' continued the lift-driver, his voice now silky, each word caressing the plush, pink walls of the lift as it escaped from his smooth, red lips. 'Designed by Mr Ernest Harridan, a member of the British Horological Society …'

And then the words were lost as the four clocks struck simultaneously, sending sickening sound waves crashing against the walls of the lift, filling Ben's senses so that his brain jangled and spun and all conscious thought was dashed from his mind …

Ben wanted to scream at the lift-driver to stop, to go up, or down—anything to get them away from the obliterating noise. His head felt like it was going to burst. It *was* bursting! Then suddenly everything settled, calmed. He took a great gulp of air and turned to the lift-driver to complain, to let him know how he felt about the hair-raising mind-trip he'd just been put through. But the words that came out of his mouth were strange, unknown to him, yet at the same time disturbingly familiar …

'… the tower rises one hundred and ninety-six metres above the ground. There are four clock faces, each five metres in diameter, with minute hands that are three metres long …'

Time Flies ◆ Meredith Costain

Ben finished the speech and looked over at the lanky teenager standing in the corner of the lift, his eyes staring insolently back under the brim of his baseball cap. He flicked a switch and the lift returned to the ground floor, the cables shuddering. The doors eased open, revealing yet another knot of day-trippers, chattering and laughing and eager to go up to the top. He watched sadly, his shoulders drooping with resignation, as the boy elbowed his way through the crowd, holding out a small black camera to a man and a woman waiting at the back of the hall. He watched, too, as the boy turned to flash him a malevolent smile before disappearing out into the sunshine.

Adjusting his peaked cap, Ben flicked yet another switch, asking if the crowd had seen the intricate plaque on the wall above the lift—whether they knew the meaning of the Latin words, *Tempus Fugit*, inscribed there.

His mouth opened and shut as if by remote control, the words about heights and weights and construction streaming endlessly out. But his mind! Inside his mind, Ben's thoughts scrabbled like a rat caught in a maze. What was it the old man had said? He'd been driven up and down in the lift by this same man for ... how many years? If he was ninety now ... Ben quickly did some calculations. At least eighty years, maybe more!

How many years would *he* be stuck here, out of the sunshine, locked up in this dreary padded cell? Eighty years? One hundred? More? Maybe if he could repeat the circumstances—wait for the right moment, get the right passenger alone in the lift at just the right time—he could turn the tables himself, and escape. But until then ...

'Yes, *tempus fugit*,' his dull voice calmly intoned to the passengers in the lift. 'It's a Latin term, meaning "time flies".'

Inwardly, however, Ben was shuddering, knowing that, for him, time might never fly again.

Missing the Last Laugh

Archimede Fusillo

Missing the Last Laugh • Archimede Fusillo

A T THE time, it sounded like a great idea. Frank, Nick and I would wait in the empty class room adjacent to Room 9B where Ms Crowley, the emergency teacher, would be taking Maths A. At some stage during the lesson, we would sneak in through the connecting door and swap places with Paul, Tim and Michael.

The swap would be easy, since there was a glass panel in the connecting door through which we could watch proceedings, and bide our time until we were sure the swap would not be noticed. The fact that Ms Crowley was near-sighted wouldn't harm the endeavour either.

We had done it before. To a student teacher who had taken our class for drama not three months earlier. He had divided the class into two equal halves, one group working in the Library, the other in the Hall. Frank, Nick and I were in the former group. Somewhere between Act 1, Scene 2 of *And The Big Men Fly* and Act 1, Scene 3, Adam, Mark and Tony disappeared, and we three took their places. Never having taken our class before, the poor man couldn't figure out why he hadn't noticed Frank's so obvious accent before.

'Tel mi hau tu do it, plis. I no rimimber,' Frank said over and over when asked to role-play the lead.

And try as he would, our emergency teacher could not get Frank to admit to the joke, and had to accept my explanation that Frank had only been in Australia a short time.

'But he does try, Sir,' I added for effect. 'All the teachers give him a go, and don't make an issue of it.'

'Non-discrimination, Sir,' put in Nick.

Mr Kutnv fixed me with his wide eyes and said softly, 'Of course, of course,' and let Frank have his say. He never told any other teacher either, except our homeroom teacher, Mr Nichols, who was conditioned enough to our ways to laugh the matter off—at least that time.

With Ms Crowley it turned out differently. Quite differently.

Ms Crowley stood very close to the board when she wrote which was a consequence of her near-sightedness. From the back she looked as though she were pressed into the blackboard itself, her entire body concentrated into a small pressure point at the tip of the blue chalk she used to identify key aspects of her discussion.

Although she had taught at our school several times before, Ms Crowley had never taken a Year Nine maths class, and what we knew about her had been gleaned from other people's accounts.

We knew, for instance, that she spoke s-l-o-w-l-y, that she always used blue chalk, and that she asked a lot of questions in class. And of course we knew she was only an emergency teacher: a passing threat of little consequence.

From behind the glass panel, the three of us watched her begin her lesson, an exposition of the merits of basic trigonometry, with bemused interest. Neither myself nor the other two were any good at maths, and that was why we were together in the woodwork class run by Mr Stewart. But he hardly ever looked up from his newspaper, and was certain not even to notice our absence.

When Ms Crowley went to the cupboard to one side of the platform to retrieve the protractor we had earlier moved there from her desk, Frank, Nick and I tiptoed in, and Paul, Tim and Michael huddled out. It was over so quickly, and so stealthily, that the boys at the front of the class didn't even look around.

By the time Ms Crowley was deep into the power of vector matrices, her questioning had begun. And soon it became Frank's turn to answer her.

Missing the Last Laugh ~ Archimede Fusillo

'You,' she said, 'what can you tell me about a single column vector?'

Frank narrowed his eyes, puffed out his cheeks, and, while the rest of us struggled not to laugh, said, 'Hu, mi?'

'You, yes,' Ms Crowley replied without a blink.

Frank looked around his class as though seeking assistance. 'Frank don't speak much English, Miss,' Nick piped up. 'He only really speaks Italian.'

'Italiano, si,' Frank smiled, 'Mi Italiano ... Yes ... plis.'

Ms Crowley squinted at Frank through her glasses. 'Then why is he in the advanced maths group?' she asked.

'Because of his brother, Miss,' Nick answered. 'That's his brother there, Miss,' he went on, pointing at me, 'Giacomo's his name. Giacomo Stucasso.'

There was a snigger around the class as everyone swallowed their laughter.

'And does the brother speak English?' Ms Crowley asked.

'Yes, Miss. He's been in Australia longer. He came out with their dad, while Frank stayed on the farm with their mother,' Nick explained quickly.

'My brother is too good for the maths, Missus,' I said, getting to my feet, gauging the play carefully. 'English, not so good.' I shrugged my shoulders and turned my hands palm up.

'And your brother can do all the work without understanding the language, is that what you'd have me believe?' Ms Crowley asked suspiciously, advancing now towards us from the platform.

'My brother listens to me for to tell him what teacher says,' I went on confidently, having played this role many times before. 'You talk, after, I talk. Then Frank he understand, Missus Crowlie.'

'Crowley ... Ms Crowley,' she corrected, drawing her mouth into a thin line.

Frank beamed a smile at her and let his eyes grow wide, begging sympathy. Behind Ms Crowley the class held their breath, laughter exploding in the depths of their bellies.

'Ask him the question I just posed, then,' Ms Crowley said.

I swallowed a grin, then looking at Frank and biding my time so as not to appear too eager, I began.

'*Franco, questa strega vuole sapere se è bella.*'

The class teetered on the brink.

Nick put one fist in his mouth to gag his laughter. Frank pondered the question: the hag wants to know if she's good-looking.

'I don't think he understand, Missus,' I said apologetically.

I don't know what I expected, but Ms Crowley just smiled, and asking me politely to sit down, returned to her desk.

In the few moments it took for her to go through some papers on her desk, Frank, Nick and I acknowledged victory with a wild gesture of our arms.

'*Franco, venga avanti, voglio spiegarti ciò che stiamo studiando.*'

The words, the accent, the confident swagger of the voice cut me down so swiftly, so completely, that for a moment I thought I'd wet my pants.

'*Dai Franco,*' Ms Crowley continued in the most rounded Italian I'd ever heard. '*Anche te, Giacomo.*'

And turning towards us, she held up a pile of class photographs, carefully labelled with the names of each student from 9B.

'You must be so new to the school,' she said sarcastically, weighing both Frank and I down with her curt grin, 'that you're not on my list, or among my photographs.'

She folded her arms stiffly and fixed the three of us with her eyes. 'Come on then,' she went on slowly, 'we'll go get your photographs from Mr Nichols, shall we.'

And with that we were marched out of the room, the others' laughter burning in our ears, haunting us even as we sat in Mr Nichols' office and he telephoned each of our parents in turn.

We were getting a three-day holiday, and no amount of begging could convince Mr Nichols otherwise.

The last we saw of Ms Crowley, she was walking back to 9B, blue chalk held gingerly between two fingers, grinning contentedly to herself.

DOING TIME

Christine Harris

Doing Time • Christine Harris

ONE wheel clips the door and Sebastian jerks sideways, his head bouncing a little. This thing's worse than a supermarket trolley.

'Thanks. I can manage now,' he says.

Fine. I stand back. I don't want to spend my afternoon pushing him around.

'I have to go to the toilet first.' He turns his head to look at me over his shoulder.

I flinch. 'I don't do toilets.'

Sebastian half-smiles. 'Who's asking?'

He pushes himself over to the wide door across the foyer.

Arms folded, I wait, wishing I was anywhere else but here. With two hands I smooth back my hair. When my fringe flops down onto my face it makes me look younger.

I sigh. This is not how I want to spend a Saturday afternoon.

I hate sport.

Cricket? It takes days to finish one game. If you can make yourself stick it out to the bitter end, you'd be smart to take a tent and a trailer-load of food.

And playing is even worse, especially when you're batting. It's like waiting for a cannonball to rearrange your face, your fingers, or something more painful. Totally uncool to roll around on the grass, curled up like a caterpillar, wondering if you'll ever be able to walk again.

Rugby? There's no fun in a bunch of meatheads tackling each other in the mud, unless you're into dirt and pain. Football? The shorts are so tight that if you make the mistake of bending over, you walk off in two halves. Table tennis? What's the point in tapping a puny lump of white plastic across a table for hours?

In my one go at table tennis I was wiped out by a snotty-nosed kid half my size. Lucky for him a table tennis bat doesn't do much damage.

Then there's tenpin bowling. The shoes are so dorky, and you don't know who's been wearing them or what's festering on their feet. And the stupid balls are so heavy that your arms are longer each time you come out of there. I cringe as I remember swinging my arm and dropping the ball with a loud crack. It rolled backwards at the speed of light. Wide-eyed people jumped left and right, except for the blonde in the stretch jeans with the loud voice. The bowling ball trundled over her left foot. And she wasn't happy, I can tell you.

Sport? No way. I shudder at the thought.

Finally Sebastian returns and I follow him outside, trotting behind like a puppy dog. His sneaker-clad feet are awfully small. The back of his red Mambo T-shirt has a picture of a devil with horns. Yeah. Right. If he's a devil, then I'm the Pope.

We move onto the oval, where a group of kids and three adults in tracksuits are gathered on the grass.

There are two metal chairs, like high chairs, with blue nylon straps pegged to the ground.

'Sebastian,' calls a woman in a tracksuit—must be the coach because she's dishing out equipment and instructions like there's no tomorrow.

'That's us,' he says to me.

'That's you, you mean.'

He looks sideways. 'You're helping, aren't you?'

I shrug.

The coach holds a silver ball in her right hand. 'Two k, Seb?'

He nods and wheels himself over to the funny-looking chair. Pushing himself up with his hands, he tries to get out of his wheelchair and onto the higher metal one and fails.

Am I supposed to lift him or leave him?

With a grunt, he tries again and heaves his body upward: made it.

The coach eyeballs me. 'Here ... er ...'

'Joel.'

'Joel,' repeats the coach, 'hold this for a second, will you?'

Abruptly, she hands me the ball and it almost rips my arms from their sockets. 'Ow.' I quickly check if anyone is watching, but they're not.

'How much does this thing weigh?'

They both grin as she straps his legs into place. 'That shotput's only two kilograms, isn't it Sebastian?'

Only?

She takes it from me and hands it to Sebastian. He leans back, his left hand gripping a metal bar, and one ... two ... three ... he hurls the silver ball into the air.

It lands with a dull thud.

I make like a tree and stand still; silent. There's no way I could throw a shotput that far. But I'm not going to tell them that.

The coach goes over to retrieve the shotput.

'What'd you do, anyway?' Sebastian asks me.

'I hit someone.' I make my voice sound hard so he won't ask any more stupid questions. 'With a cricket bat.'

He doesn't take the hint. 'Why?'

'Because I couldn't find a shotput,' I smirk.

Looking down at him, I feel too tall, almost gigantic. His brown eyes are friendly, curious.

'I don't do conversation,' I say, shutting the door on further revelations.

'That was a good shot, Sebastian.' A girl with braces pushes herself up close. Her wheelchair is psycho with colour; looks like she whizzed through a paint shop. Then she pushes off to peer at a peacock-blue chair, then a red one. What does she think this is, a chairmart?

If Sebastian can ask nosy questions about my community service hours, I can ask him something. 'What's the matter with you, anyway?'

He looks at me sideways. 'Don't worry, nothing contagious.'

I squat beside him so he can see I'm not scared of germs. Besides, I feel guilty towering over him on my legs.

'I've got spina bifida.' He sees that I haven't got a clue what he's on about. 'My brain doesn't give messages to my legs, so they don't work.'

A little way off, the coach is waylaid by a kid complaining about a javelin. 'It's a boomerang. This thing's so bent it comes back by itself. It bends if you look at it.'

In a soft voice, the coach shows the kid how to hold it properly. 'It'll stick in your hand if you grip it like that. Why don't you get out in the paddock at home and practise with a broomstick?'

A fair-haired woman, probably his mother, yells out, 'He's got a javelin. It's under his bed.'

With a laugh, the coach pats his shoulder. 'Is that where you keep your shotpot?'

The kid laughs; the mother laughs; the coach laughs. I yawn.

I look at Sebastian, perched precariously on the metal chair, then at some of the other kids. 'You ever fall out of your wheelchair?'

He nods. 'Sometimes.'

'Backwards or forwards?'

'Backwards, forwards and sideways.'

His eyes are alight with amusement, whether at himself or me, I'm not sure.

'How can you fall sideways?'

'Some kids at school pressed the buttons on my wheels.'

I look at the wheels on his vacant chair—can't see anything special. 'Is that the brake?'

He shakes his head. 'No. If you press the button in the middle, the wheel comes off. So you can put the chair in the car. These kids pressed the button and I didn't know. When I tried to move my chair, the wheel fell off, and so did I.'

Indignant on his behalf, I think how humiliating it would be to crash in a heap like that, especially if you couldn't get back up again without help.

'Did you get those kids back?'

'Nah. They're my friends. And once I was doing an obstacle race at the junior games and I hit a piece of wood and went for a six. Got a beaut egg on the back of my head.'

This I can't work out. 'Why do you keep doing this then?'

Without looking at me, his voice steady, he says, 'I want to win.'

There is a small silence between us.

'But you can't always win,' I say. 'What if you mess up?'

'I have another go,' he answers with a shrug.

At last, the coach returns with the heavy shotput and Sebastian chucks it a second time. It goes a little further.

'Don't you want it?' the coach jokes. 'Every time I give it to you, you throw it away.'

Her sense of humour is really bad. I don't know if Sebastian laughs because he thinks it's funny or because he feels sorry for her.

I pluck at a blade of grass. 'Are you any good at this stuff?'

'I've got six medals. I eat vegetables, so I'm fairly strong.'

Medals? What use are they? You wouldn't get much for them. Also, I hate vegetables, and tell him so.

'Me too, but I meant that I can eat vegetables.' He nods towards the other kids. 'Some of them can't swallow properly.'

For a second, I feel really stupid.

'You're lucky, you know,' he says.

For a moment, I assume he means my legs.

Then he adds, 'I read about someone who had to do community service in a chicken factory. He plucked feathers from an eagle at a zoo. The judge said if he liked feathers so much, he could have all he wanted.'

I suppose a month helping out at wheelchair sports is better than doing time in a chicken factory. Actually, I didn't really hurt the guy I thumped—only his pride. He'd had bruises before, much worse than the one I gave him. And he'd started it. Giving me heaps like that, especially in front of Jane-Marie Yates. The sound of her sniggers lit a fire inside me that only went out with the sound of the wood connecting with his skull.

Sebastian's cough brings me back to the present.

'You want a rug or anything?' I ask, wondering if he feels the cold. 'A drink or …?'

He turns his eyes on me, and says in a good-natured way, 'Chill out.'

My mouth falls open.

'Don't pamper me. I'm not a poodle. It reminds me that I'm in a wheelchair …'

How could he forget he's in a wheelchair?

'Anyway … being polite doesn't suit you. Just be normal.'

Ha. If I was being 'normal' I wouldn't be here. I'd be down the mall, checking out babes.

'Good on ya, Tony!' The whole bunch clap and shout as the tape measure comes out and a boy with thick glasses grins like his face will split in half.

'He's a new kid,' says Sebastian and, without pausing, adds, 'want a ride?'

Astonished, I blink. 'In the chair?'

Sebastian nods. 'It'll cost you though.'

'What?'

'Five dollars.'

As if I'd pay some guy to slip into his warm chair for a burn around the oval.

Sebastian says, 'When I was in primary school I got heaps of money from the others. Then the teacher made me stop because kids were losing their bus money.'

I shake my head. 'I don't do chairs.'

What if someone saw me? I have a reputation to worry about.

But I guess there would be some benefits to a wheelchair. You could get away with a lot. People would feel sorry for you—and you wouldn't get a judge giving you dumb community service.

'You ever walked?' I ask.

'Sometimes I dream about it.' He shrugs just once, his face a mixture of puzzlement and yearning. 'I can't feel it, though. It's like a movie, only I can see myself. I just wish I could feel it. You tell me, what's it like to be an upright?'

I'd been calling him a wheelie in my head, but it gives me a start when he calls me an upright. It makes me sound like a hairy shuffling animal that's escaped from a science lab. What's it like to walk? I find I can't describe it. It's just something you do. You never think about it.

'It feels … tall.' I'm not satisfied with my answer but it's all I can think of.

He nods as though I've said something really profound.

Doing Time • Christine Harris

I shift uncomfortably then sit on the grass, hoping I won't get green stains on my new jeans.

A breeze rushes across the oval. I brush back my hair.

'How about javelin now?' asks the coach.

So that the kid with the thick glasses can use the special chair, Sebastian struggles back into his wheelchair. It's easier going down than up.

He points to the javelin and I pick it up for him. He tests the weight in his right hand and grips it near the centre. 'You can't look at the ground, or it falls short. You have to look up at the sky and imagine the javelin flying over the top of the trees.'

Sebastian's face is full of concentration. Is he imagining the javelin, or himself, flying over the trees?

One ... two ... three.

With a sudden swing of his arm, he hurls the javelin. Up, up it flies toward the sky then arcs down and the tip stabs the earth, wobbling a few times before it's still.

Way longer than all the other throws, it's a ripper.

'Yay.' I start to clap, then falter, embarrassed at my show of enthusiasm.

I feel my face go red and I try to look bored. But still, a little knot of excitement stays in my stomach. That javelin flew like a bird.

'Well, you going to get it for me, or what?' We exchange glances and I know he's trying to distract me from my awkwardness.

I fetch the javelin, feeling its sleekness in my hand.

'Have a go,' he says.

'No ...' I want to say more but can't.

'Go on.'

All these people here—what if I look stupid?

I shake my head. 'I'll mess up. I always do.'

Sebastian, chin resting on one hand, looks up at me from his wheelchair. 'So?'

He's got a bung back; he's on wheels; he has to chat up girls from a sitting position—but I'm the one that feels clumsy.

Sebastian's brown eyes dare me to try. I remember how I felt watching his throw.

'Did it hurt when you fell out of your chair in the obstacle race?' I ask.

'Like hell.' Sebastian faces the oval. 'But I don't care too much if I fall over. The crowd's going to be cheering when I win. Now, you aim for that tree over there.' He points to a huge gum tree on the far side.

'Oh sure.' I roll my eyes but I don't put down the javelin.

I aim for the sky just above the tree and hurl the javelin with all my strength. It barely gets any air under it and, instead of soaring majestically upward, skims over the ground and flops.

'You looked at the ground,' says Sebastian.

Hands on hips, I glare at him. 'Did not. I looked at the top of the tree, like you said.'

He laughs at me, and I don't mind, which surprises me. His chuckles are kind of friendly.

'First time I threw a javelin I forgot to look behind and when I drew my arm back, I hit a kid on the head. Lucky it only grazed him. Gave him a fright, though. Don't worry. You'll get better with practice.'

An image of a bowling ball rolling backwards flashes through my mind.

I avoid his eyes so I don't start laughing too. 'I don't do practice,' I say.

But this time I don't really mean it.

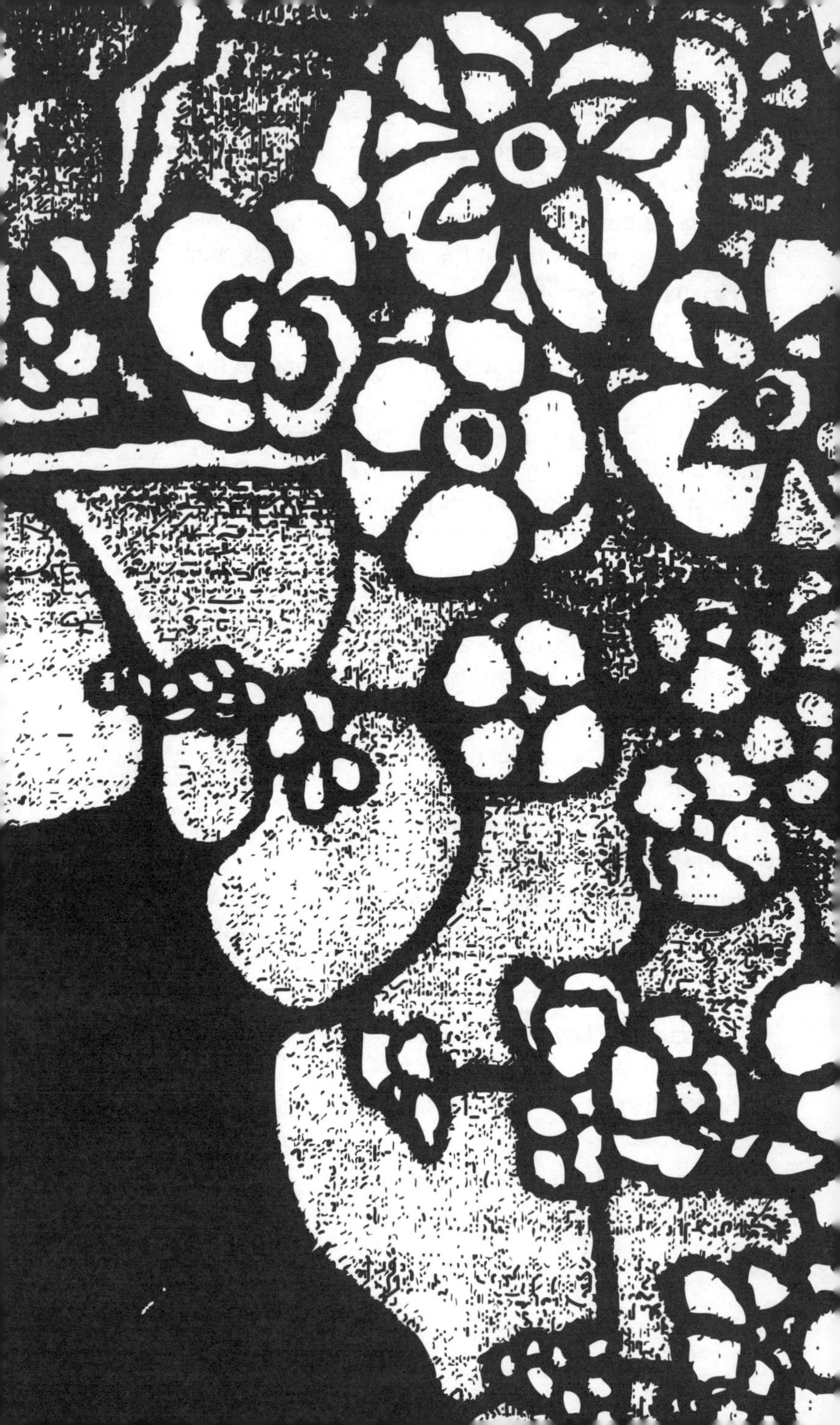

SMUDGE

Jackie French

Smudge • Jackie French

I AM not sure when I met him, maybe because he was always there.

I sat in the yellow grass above the creek where the valley's first sunlight slanted through a gap in the cliffs, making thermals for the wedge-tailed eagles to glide on, and he grazed on the creek flat or pulled at tussocks around me, till finally one morning he ate beside me, a large sandy-coloured wombat with a smudge across one ear.

'Hello, wombat,' I said.

The wombat ignored me. He pulled another mouthful of grass.

'You're a smudged wombat,' I said. 'Smudge the wombat.' Smudge sniffed once and went on eating.

I walked back to the shed, carrying my empty muesli bowl. Smudge sniffed again, as though to work out which way I'd gone. Then he went back to his grass.

I lived in a shed in those days, mostly by myself. The neighbours were about half an hour's walk away. I still didn't have the truck, or running water, unless you counted the creek. I swam there every evening after I'd soaped myself clean on the bank so the soap didn't go in the water. (Wombats don't like drinking soapy water. Neither do I.) The water was so cold my scalp felt like it was crawling off my head when I washed my hair and the soap scum glistened on the grass.

Sometimes at night I lit the kerosene lantern. Mostly I didn't bother. I'd grown to like starlight and shadows and, anyway, most nights aren't really dark.

The moon crept down between the casuarinas as I went to bed. I could see moon shadows through the window, silver shadows, not at all like the sun's. The bush rats scampered across the rafters as I went to sleep, dropping apricot stones onto the concrete below to crack them for the kernel inside.

Something woke me. It was louder than the clunking apricot stones. It was a tearing sound somewhere behind my left ear ... tchopp tchopp tchopp.

I know what that is, I thought. It's a monster creeping up from the creek to eat me in my bed.

And then I thought, No, monsters usually don't go tchopp tchopp tchopp.

I opened my eyes, but the moon no longer shone through the window. The room was dark.

I sat up. The tearing sound moved closer, louder, almost like the sound of someone munching ... tchopp tchopp tchopp ...

I opened the door. The moonlight was black and silver. So was the wombat.

'Hello Smudge,' I said.

Smudge peered up at me. Wombats are short-sighted. They can only see what's right under their noses. After all, for a wombat, that's what's important—the grass and dirt at nose level, not what's happening in the world a metre or two away.

Smudge sniffed again as though to be sure it was me. Then he sniffed the grass in front to find the sweetest. He went back to eating. Tchopp tchopp tchopp.

I went back to bed.

An hour later something crashed against the door.

Bang, scratch, bang!

'All right, I'm coming.'

Bang, scratch, bang.

'Hold on, you stupid marsupial ...'

I opened the door.

Smudge blinked and padded into the shed. He'd known I was in there somewhere. If you're a wombat and can't find the entrance, you dig one, or break the door down.

'This is a door,' I said. 'It opens. I know wombats can't open doors, but if you'd waited properly after knocking, I would have come.'

Smudge ignored me. He stopped at the cupboard first, as though to show me he knew all about doors now. He sniffed it, then pawed it vigorously.

'You want to look in there, right?'

No comment from the wombat.

I opened the door.

Smudge sniffed around the entrance carefully, then sniffed once more inside. He shoved his nose onto the shelf.

'Hey, you're not supposed to go in there. That's where I keep my saucepans.'

Smudge ignored me.

He shoved the frying pan aside with his nose, then thrust it backwards with his hind legs as it fell out.

Crash!

'Hey, watch out, you'll break it! No—leave the kettle alone …'

I started to grab him, then stopped. What part of a wombat do you grab? Wombats are built like hairy tanks. They're mostly hair and muscle.

Did wombats bite? Of course they did. I remembered a zoo keeper friend who'd had his knee ripped open by a wombat. They got more injuries from wombats in that zoo, he said, than all the tigers, rhinoceri and dingoes put together.

I watched Smudge's bum disappear into the cupboard. A saucepan crashed beside me, and then its lid. The camp oven needed three separate shoves. A plastic sieve crumpled at the door. And then his face appeared, triumphant. I saw a wombat grin for the first time.

To Smudge the cupboard was just another wombat hole—a messy one that I'd never got round to cleaning up. He'd emptied it for me. It was nice and tidy now. I could crawl inside and sleep there if I wanted to.

'Thanks. I think,' I said. Smudge plodded over to check under the bed, under the table, under the pot-belly stove.

He didn't say goodnight. Unlike dogs, humanised after thousands of years of contact, wombats don't make a ceremony of leaving. You're either there, or else you're not. And if you're not there's nothing to bother about ... Smudge just left.

I heard the munching from behind the shed again. Then I went back to bed.

Smudge was at the creek flat when I went out for breakfast. He was still eating. I wondered if he'd run away from me, in the daylight. Smudge sniffed, then froze, the way wombats do before they gallop off to safety.

'It's me,' I said. 'Remember me?'

Smudge recognised my voice. I kept speaking as I came closer so he'd know who made the noise. 'I woke up late, that's all. Some furry lump disturbed my sleep and tossed out all my saucepans. It took me hours to get back to sleep ...'

Smudge sat on the grass beside me. He gave one final sniff just to be sure it wasn't an impostor, borrowing my voice.

He sniffed again—my knee, my ankle, deep inside my boot.

'You'll get your whiskers stuck.'

Smudge sniffed my other boot, then up to my knee. He seemed to think he'd sniffed enough. He sat beside me, close enough to touch, and seemed to go to sleep.

I looked at him more closely. He wasn't asleep. His eyes were almost open. He looked content, feeling the soft morning sun, the breeze between the trees. We sat together on the warm soil, the shadows on our faces.

The day grew hotter. Smudge opened his eyes and marched into the trees. It was time to retreat to the coolness of his burrow. I wondered if he assumed I'd have the sense to do the same. But maybe not. Smudge always seemed to accept that we were different.

Night comes early to the valley. The shadows thicken as the sun falls behind the trees. The top of the ridge turns to flames as the sun sets behind it. In winter, wombats come outside with shadow fall; in summer they come out when the air grows cooler.

Wallabies come out at dusk and sniff the air. Scents change with dusk as well. The hot air rises from the valley and cooler air sinks down. There's always wind at dusk at this end of the valley; only daytime is ever truly still.

I used to sing with the wind at dusk, when I lived alone.

I sang by the creek that night, on a tall rock smoothed by a thousand floods. The shadows turned into the darkness. A bandicoot hopped between the casuarina roots and began to dig. A wallaby nosed for watercress between the rocks, a blacker form in the dark. Another darker lump came a little closer, and then much closer still.

'Hello,' I said. 'It's you.'

Smudge pulled a bit of tussock. He'd known my voice and had come to listen.

He followed me when I went up the path towards the shed. I left the door open to listen to his chomping outside, while I chopped vegetables for dinner.

It was lonely when the sound of his munching died away. I turned the lamp off and went outside. Smudge was a dark shape down by the creek. His ears flicked as he heard my footsteps, then he went back to eating—early evening eating is a serious job for wombats. Nothing trivial interrupts it.

I sat on a rock and watched him as he grazed his way along the flat, then up onto the hillside. He stopped there for a while. Another wombat padded by. It paused a nose length from Smudge and sniffed. Smudge sniffed, too. The new wombat sniffed my way. Smudge growled something—maybe establishing his territory, which included me, or just reassuring the newcomer I was okay to have around. The new wombat peered through the dark, then padded down the path.

Smudge kept on walking, pausing once to leave a dropping on a rock. Any minute I expected him to scramble down a hole, but he didn't. He stopped, finally, halfway up the ridge and settled into a grassy hollow.

I moved closer to him. I wondered if he'd forgotten I was there. He didn't move. I think he'd taken my presence for granted all along.

I sat down beside him. This was his spot, his evening sitting place, as the knoll where I had breakfast was mine.

I looked out over the valley.

Colours are different at night. They are purple colours, grey and green and blue colours, not the red and yellow of the day. The night was light enough for shadow, though the moon was still hovering behind the ridge. The world was glittery with starlight so bright that when you watched only the stars for five minutes it was hard to see shapes on the darker earth below.

I don't know how long we sat there. The moon rose. A tide of moonlight crept down from the ridge opposite, then up towards us, till we were covered with its light as well. Smudge got to his feet and trotted down the path, back to the creek. He began to eat.

I didn't stay with him all night that time, though other nights I did. I think it was with Smudge that I really discovered the bush. I'd walked in it before, but always going to somewhere. I never had time to watch.

I was usually with other people, too. The bush is different when you're with people. It becomes a human place. Things just aren't quite ... the same ... when you're with other people.

But even by myself during the day I had something that I meant to do—prune trees or collect seeds, or just climb from one ridge to the next to see what was beyond.

The nights with Smudge were timeless. I simply smelt the night.

※

The apricots were late that year. The summer mist drifted up the valley every afternoon, so the ground cooled like the air. It was Christmas before the apricots were really sweet.

Smudge liked apricots. At first he ate the half-green ones the wind blew off the trees. Then he got fussy. He nosed among the tussocks looking for the most perfect ones. He glared at the wallaby that sat under the tree with him. The wallaby was a glutton. It ate every apricot it could find.

Smudge was a connoisseur.

He savoured each apricot. His chin got stickier and his droppings smelt of fruit.

I carried boxes up to the top orchard, well away from Smudge's territory, and lugged them back full of apricots. I spent the afternoons slicing them and spreading them to dry on long strips of reflective insulation. Smudge sat with me as the shadows joined together. He sniffed the fruit, wondering what I was doing, then ignored it, dozing on the mist-cooled ground.

The fruit dried slowly, heating and drying up a little each morning, then dampening again in the afternoon. I took them inside the first night so they didn't get too wet; on the second night, too. The third night they seemed dry enough to leave outside all night. I reckoned they'd be ready in another day or two.

I went out to inspect them on the fourth morning. At least half of them had gone. An empty path lay there like a vacuum cleaner had wandered through sucking up every one in front of it.

Smudge didn't appear at breakfast, or that night, or the next. He returned the night after that, but he wasn't interested in the apricot tree. He turned his back on it and stuck to grass.

❧

Winter moves slowly into the valley. The ground cools gradually. It's not till the first icy wind travels down the gorge that you realise summer's gone. The days darken suddenly after that, with clear, cold afternoons full of chilly light.

Smudge liked the afternoons. He wandered out an hour before shadow fall, sniffing for the warmest, driest place. Sometimes he made a nest in the long grass. I'd find him dozing, his eyes shut against the light. Other times he dust-bathed, wriggling in the bare spots in the track made by the truck, till the dirt was soft and warm about him. Most times he'd lie there, front paws stretched out and dust up to his armpits; or he'd roll onto his back, his fluffy stomach soaking up the heat.

I think he slept during the coldest part of the night. I don't know. I stayed inside at night for those months too.

Sometime that winter I scraped up enough money to buy a tape deck, powered by an old car battery. I turned the volume up to drown out the wind, the creaking roof, the squeaks of the bush rats as they scuttled across the rafters, then went outside to get some water.

'Urrp ...' I said, as I tripped over something large sitting on the doorstep.

It was Smudge.

I thought he was asleep. Normally he butted at the door if he wanted to come in. But he was listening.

I've never known another wombat who liked music.

Smudge preferred Mozart, though he was very fond of Bach. He didn't mind sixteenth century dances either, although five minutes of rock'n'roll on the radio was enough to send him back down to the creek. I avoided rock music after that. But mostly Smudge's likes were the same as mine.

Still deeper into winter I bought a violin with money from the cauliflower crop. It was the first time I'd had a violin since I was a teenager. It was the first time I'd played since then, too, and it sounded like possums sliding down the roof. But Smudge seemed to like it. He sat on the doorstep and twitched his nose, and peered inside to see what had happened whenever I took a break.

Smudge is the only creature who, human or marsupial, ever liked my violin playing. But maybe he was only being kind.

There was no rain that winter, apart from a few drops dried by the wind before they hit the ground. The valley grew drier.

Summer came, suddenly; hot, dry winds and clear, round skies, like a balloon had been stretched over the valley, so high and tight you felt that you could prick it with a pin and maybe water would come pouring out.

The sky stayed cloudless.

Clouds appeared finally, thin high drifts, then drifted off again. The grass crackled like cornflakes underfoot. The ground was hot and hard.

I watered the vegetable garden and the grass around the shed. The magpies danced and spread their wings in the spray, two magpies, four, then forty, fifty—a whole parliament of magpies, yelling in the branches and dancing in the water.

Only one thunderstorm in December; hail on New Year's Day. Enough to rip off leaves and wet the soil, not enough to soak and feed the grass. No other rain. Autumn was dry. The animals were thin.

Smudge was unchanged. He had the grass around the shed. I let him forage in the vegetable garden now, leaving the gate open for an hour or two at dusk, keeping an eye open for wallabies who'd devastate the corn and trample the tomatoes.

Smudge ignored the vegetables. He liked the young oats that sprang up from the mulch, and the more succulent weeds. He left droppings by the lettuces, furry with digested grass. The native dung beetles decomposed them before the sun was high the next day.

Another dry winter, then a summer I hate to remember. The springs dried up on the hills. The grass shrivelled leaving concrete ground.

Starving animals wandered from the ridges; skeleton wallabies that tore at the shelters round the trees till their hands were bloody, desperate for anything green; wombats, all ribs and thin, pale fur, mad with mange and thirst and heat, who plunged into the smelly puddles of the creek or tried to bury themselves in the damp sand.

There was enough water for the garden. I bucketed a little to the trees. I grew more oats for Smudge—deliberately now. He foraged in the damp spots in the creek. He was greyer and thinner. I was thinner, too. We both abandoned daylight now—I worked and watered in the grey light in the morning or at dusk.

I spent my nights with Smudge. The bush looked softer at night. You couldn't see the trees dying on the ridge.

Smudge grew slower and thinner, though I don't think it was starvation. Finally, he lay under the corn, and slept most of the day, eating a few mouthfuls at night, then sleeping again. By the third day he was panting. He was obviously in pain.

I sat with him the fourth day and through the night. He died on the fifth day. He's buried where he died at one end of the vegetable garden, though I haven't grown vegetables there since. My vegetable garden now is across the creek from the old shed and grazed by other wombats.

I don't think the drought killed him. He was an old wombat when I first met him. I doubt there was anything a vet could have done. In those days most vets knew nothing about wombats.

I moved to the new shed across the creek soon after Smudge's death, leaving the flat to Moriarty, the wombat who took over his territory. Smudge's apricot trees dried in the drought. Ants have made a giant nest under one of them.

I planted out Smudge's garden with asparagus and rhubarb, which doesn't need much looking after. It was too far away to maintain when I moved across the creek.

The new shed gradually turned into my house. No one who sees it now would realise it had once been a shed. Sometimes weeks go by without one of us going over to Smudge's flat and the old shed, except in asparagus season, or when the navel oranges are ripe.

There were other wombats living round the new shed when I moved into it; Sneezy and Lurk and the Golden Dragon. They accepted me and after a time no longer ran away.

Over the years we've adopted orphaned wombats, too, and raised them till they could go back to the bush. But a wombat who has grown up with humans from when it is a baby is different from a wild wombat offering you friendship.

Smudge was perhaps the closest friend I've ever had; but he wasn't a human and the friendship wasn't like human friendships. It takes a courageous wombat to have a human for a friend.

I have never again been as close to a wombat as I was with Smudge. Maybe you can't really be close to a wild animal when you live in a house. The doors are shut against the sun and wind; we've got electric light now to keep away the night while the wombats munch by moonlight outside.

But ...

A few years ago I walked up from the vegetable garden at dusk, carrying an armload of silver beet for dinner. My son, Edward, was crouched under the apple trees. There was someone with him. It was hard to make them out in the dark.

I put down the silver beet and came closer. Edward looked up at me, then back at his companion, shadow-like under the apples.

The shadow moved. It was a wombat, the largest I've ever seen. He had a blunt nose and silver whiskers, and long, soft ears that swivelled as I approached.

'His name's Chocolate,' said Edward, offering another carrot to the wombat. Chocolate took the carrot, holding it firmly against the ground with one large paw while he crunched it, starting at the middle and grinding at both sides.

'He likes carrots,' said Edward. 'He doesn't like celery much though.'

Chocolate looked embarrassed and a bit uncertain, as though to say, 'I don't know quite what's happening, but I think it's nice.' He finished the carrot, sniffed Edward's boots, then wandered back into the shadow of the apple trees.

Chocolate comes back often now, though not every night. I've gone for a walk with him a couple of times, while Edward is reading or watching videos, but Chocolate is Edward's friend. They sit together up on the grass above the roses, Edward's arm around Chocolate's shoulders, and Chocolate munching or simply listening … as if they are communicating.

I learnt with Smudge that conversations with a wombat simply can't be translated.

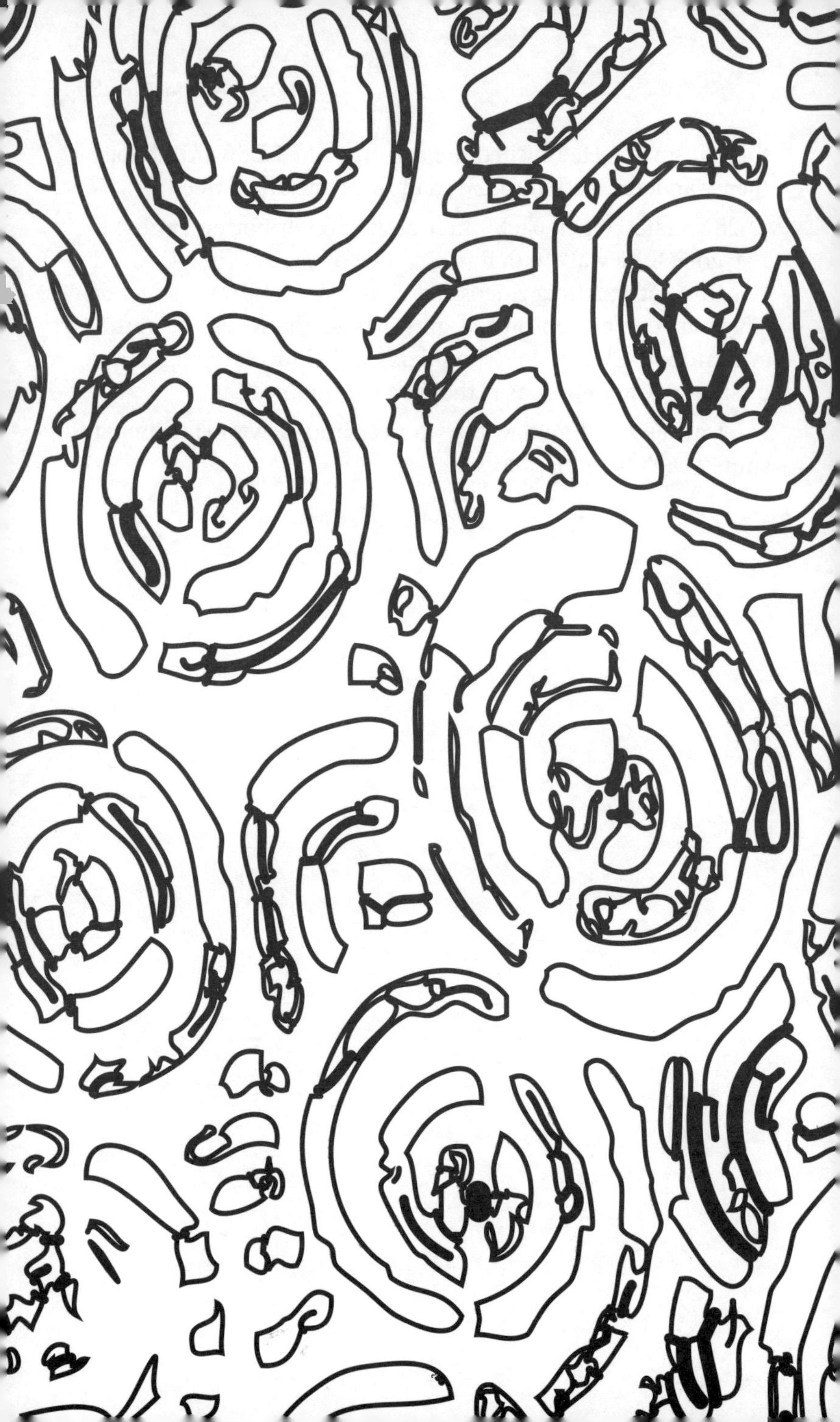

HAUNTED

Victor Kelleher

Haunted ❦ Victor Kelleher

HERE is what Susie did at bedtime every night. She tiptoed into her darkened room, ran quickly across the carpet, and jumped into bed. She never dared look under the bed. She didn't let so much as a toe stick out over the edge. Her big sister had told her what would happen if she did. Something might reach up from below and grab her. Something might tug her out of bed and pull her down and down into the ...

But it was too scary to imagine. She had heard stories about the ghosts and monsters that hid under beds, and she never wanted to meet one. She didn't even want to think about them. With a shiver, she clenched her eyes shut and went straight to sleep.

❦

In that very same room, here is what Giffin did every night. He tiptoed from a darkened corner, hurried across the carpet, and dived *under* the bed. He never dared peek out. He didn't let so much as the tip of his nose show. His big brother had told him what would happen if he did. Something might reach down and grab him. Something might tug him out from under the bed and pull him up and up into ...

But it was too scary to imagine. He had heard stories about horrible humans who slept on the top of beds. He certainly never wanted to meet one. He didn't even want to think about them. With a shudder, he opened his eyes wider than ever and didn't sleep a wink.

❦

Things stayed that way for months and months. Then early one morning, just before dawn, everything changed. As the clock in the passage struck five, Susie's eyes flicked open. She was suddenly wide awake.

At exactly the same moment, Giffin's eyes clicked shut. He was suddenly fast asleep.

So there they were. Susie on top of the bed, staring into the dark. Giffin underneath it, sleeping peacefully down amongst the dust and balls of fluff.

He was snoring too!

It was his snoring that frightened Susie. Every time he breathed in, it was like the howling of hungry wolves. Every time he breathed out, it was like the clanking of rusty chains. She'd never been so scared in all her life. She tried hiding under the blankets, but the creepy noises floated up through the mattress. She tried blocking her ears, but his snores still made the bed tremble.

She was trembling by then. She couldn't even get her voice to work properly. 'H-e-l-p!' she croaked, and made a dash for the door. But her feet tangled in the sheet, and she fell with a crash.

ત&

The noise woke Giffin. He could hear someone crying and moaning. Every time she sobbed, it was like a stab of burning sunshine. Every time she moaned, it was like an icy wash of morning light. He'd never been so scared in all his afterlife. He tried huddling in amongst the fluff-balls, but the terrible noises floated down through the mattress. He tried blocking his ears, but her sobs still made the floor tremble.

He was trembling too by then. He couldn't even get his voice to work properly. 'H-e-l-p!' he jibbered, and made a dash for the darkest corner. But his feet slipped on the fluff-balls, and he fell with a splat.

ત&

That was when Susie saw it: a ghostly white blob with wide staring eyes. It was gazing at her through the dark.

That was when Giffin also saw it: a solid pinkish blob. It was gazing back at him.

'Wh-wh-who are y-y-you?' asked Susie in a terrified whisper.

'Wh-wh-who are *y-y-you*?' asked Giffin in a hollow voice.

'M-m-my name is S-s-susie. I'm a p-p-person.'

'M-m-my name is G-g-giffin. I'm a g-g-ghost.'

Once they'd admitted the awful truth, it didn't seem so awful any more. Susie even noticed that Giffin's soft white body was rather nice to look at. It reminded her of silvery moonlight. And Giffin noticed that Susie's soft brown hair was rather beautiful. It reminded him of shadows stirred gently by the night wind.

'What are you doing in my room?' Giffin wondered aloud.

'What are you doing in *my* room?' Susie corrected him.

In his creakiest voice, he explained how he had always lived in this same room in this same house with the same ghostly family. When he had finished, Susie explained how she and her family lived there as well.

Giffin was shocked. 'You mean our house is haunted by humans?'

'And ours by ghosts?' Susie added.

Round about then, dawn started to break. As the first grey light stole into the room, Susie noticed something peculiar happening. Giffin's eyes were growing dimmer by the moment; and the round blob of his body began fading away.

'Giffin!' she said, surprised. 'Where are you going?'

'Susie!' he called back, as she also began to fade. 'Where are *you* going?'

Frantically, they reached for each other. They had forgotten about being afraid of creatures that might grab them in the dark. All they wanted now was to keep each other there.

But Susie's hand swept only empty space. And Giffin's brushed nothing more solid than shadows.

'Come back!' Susie pleaded, as sunlight peeped through a gap in the curtains.

'Come back!' she heard Giffin reply, his voice fainter than the creak of a distant door.

With a sigh, Susie lay down amongst the tangled bedclothes. She was lying there still, fast asleep, when her mum came to wake her later that morning.

'My goodness!' she exclaimed. 'What a racket you were making in the night. Anyone would think you'd seen a ghost.'

At the very same instant, up in the gloomy old attic, a far spookier voice was saying, 'My badness! What a noise you made last night. Anyone would think you'd seen a human.'

Susie and Giffin smiled a secret smile.

'Maybe I did,' they answered together.

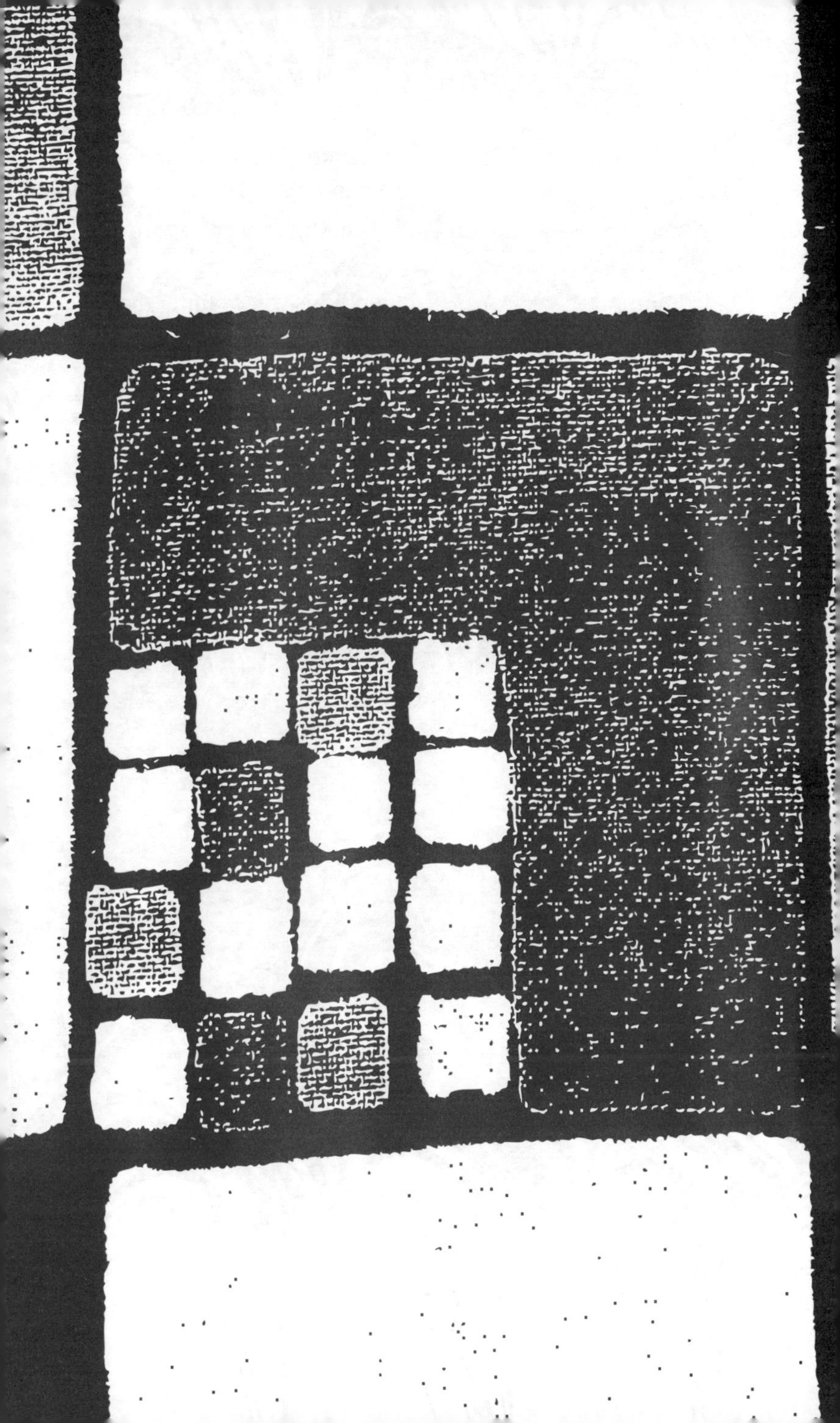

A Dolphin Dream

Gillian Rubinstein

A Dolphin Dream • Gillian Rubinstein

L IZZIE hardly cried at all when her father died. Everyone said it would have been much better if she had. But she was only eight, and it was as though she couldn't grasp what had happened. She seemed to be more puzzled than anything, puzzled and rather angry as though he had let her down by dying. She started waking at night and wandering into her mother's room and saying in a sharp questioning voice, 'Daddy? Daddy?'

Her mother found this much more unnerving than tears. Lara, who was three years older, cried extravagantly, as she always did everything, and the weeping helped to lessen the dreadful pain of loss. But Lizzie did not cry; instead she became angry and fearful as well as pale and thin.

Once school ended for the summer, none of them could bear the thought of Christmas without Dad.

'I wish we could go to the peninsula,' Lara said one morning, looking wearily at her cereal. Lizzie was still sleeping, having woken them up several times in the night.

Mum was about to drink a mouthful of tea. Instead she stopped with the cup halfway to her lips, and gazed thoughtfully at Lara. 'That's just what I was thinking last night! Would you really like to? I think it would be so good for us all to get away, but you know how much Dad loved it over there. I'm afraid it will bring back too many memories.'

'Everything here brings back too many memories anyway,' Lara pointed out, blinking hard. 'At least there there'll be a bit more space around them.'

Now she had started thinking about it she was filled with longing, as though the wide sweep of the bay, the white empty

A Dolphin Dream ~ Gillian Rubinstein

dunes and the turquoise water held some power that would heal her. Perhaps Mum felt the same thing. She put down her tea, gave Lara a grin that was nearly as good as her old ones, and jumped up from the table.

'Come on, Lara; let's get going. You get the camping list, and get the gear together. I'll organise the food.'

Getting on the road was as exciting as ever, and Lara found that she could almost forget about her father for a little while. When they were away from home his death did not seem so final, more like he had gone on a trip and would be back in a few days. Her grief lifted and, when they came to the end of the four-hour journey, and the Subaru nosed carefully but firmly onto the white sands of the bay, she gave a hoot of excitement.

They set up camp in the dunes, putting up the tent and the cooking annexe, organising the eskies, the stove and the water bottles. Lara had never realised how much work there was to do, and Mum was looking exhausted by the time it was all finished, especially since Lizzie was being no help at all. She seemed to be getting angrier and angrier, and she shouted at her sister when Lara asked her to hold a rope.

'What's the matter with you?' Lara said. 'You've got to help a little bit, since Dad's not here.'

'Where is he?' Lizzie shouted even louder. 'I thought he was going to be here! I thought that was why we came!' Her face was red and angry, and her eyes were bright, but the tears were tears of rage, and anyway they remained unshed.

'Oh darling,' Mum said. 'Daddy's not here. He's dead. He died in the car accident.'

A Dolphin Dream • Gillian Rubinstein

When they unpacked the swimming gear something at the bottom of the bag caught Lara's eye.

'Look, Mum,' she exclaimed, pulling it out. 'It's Dad's shell necklace!'

It was a short string of white shells that her father had worn on the beach, telling the children it was his last souvenir of the days when he was a surfie. Lara gazed at it sadly. It brought back such strong memories of him, she could almost feel him next to her. It seemed so strange that the necklace should still be here while he was not. It was too precious a thing to put back in the bag, so she put it round her own neck, where it lay cool against the brown skin, just above her collar bones. Then she cried again, and so did Mum, and the unpacking had to be interrupted while they held each other. But Lizzie ran away up the beach and threw stones at rocks.

Finally everything was done. Mum boiled up a kettle of water on the gas stove and made a cup of tea. She and Lara looked proudly at the little camp. They both felt a strong satisfaction and relief that they had done it on their own. They had taken another step without him. They were sad, but they were going to survive.

'We'll make a fire on the beach later,' Mum said, 'and cook sausages and beans on it. But why don't we have a swim now, while it's still warm?'

Lara and Lizzie ran down to the water with their face masks and snorkels. Lara dived straight in, but when she surfaced through the clear, sparkling water, Lizzie was still standing on the edge.

Mum came up to her and took her hand gently. 'Come on, darling, we'll go in together.' But Lizzie twisted away.

'I don't want to go in! There are too many crabs!'

A Dolphin Dream — Gillian Rubinstein

When she was little she had been terrified of crabs. Dad used to carry her into the sea so she did not have to put her feet on the sand. Last summer she had walked in through the wavelets fearlessly. Now, however, the crabs seemed to have returned.

'Don't be such a sook, Lizzie,' Lara called meanly. She was afraid Lizzie was going to spoil the holiday, and she hated seeing the sad, worried look that came into Mum's eyes every time Lizzie got difficult.

'Just stay on the edge, then,' Mum said. 'I must get in the water or I'll die!'

She and Lara swam together, following shoals of fish across the clean smooth sand into enchanted worlds of rocks and seaweed. When they looked up to check on Lizzie she was up by the high-water mark, strolling along, head down, eyes on the ground, stopping every few steps to crouch down and examine something on the beach.

'She's a strandlooper,' Lara said, hoping to see Mum smile. It was their father's word, one that he had gleaned from some book or other and handed on to them: *strandlooper*, the strange ancient race that once lived on the South African coast and loved beautiful shells.

Mum did smile. 'I hope she's finding some treasures to cheer her up.'

When they came out of the water and ran back to the camp to wrap themselves in their towels, Lizzie had arranged her treasures in a little hollow in the dunes. Around the edge was a circle of pipi shells, bleached white and mauve streaked, broken up every now and then by a shiny grey oyster with craggy white edges. In the middle was a most unusual bone, like a cross or a four-pointed star. There were lines radiating out from the centre almost as though it had been carved, and when Lara picked it up to look at it more closely she could see that there were holes in it, as though it had once hung on a string around someone's neck.

'What is it, Mum?'

Mum took it from her. 'I think it's some sort of vertebra—part of the backbone.' She ran her hand down the knobbles on Lara's spine. 'But I don't know what sort of animal it's from.' She put it back carefully in the centre of the circle. 'It's lovely, Lizzie. You were clever to find such a treasure!'

Lizzie smiled a little then. 'It's mine,' she said proudly. 'I found it!'

'You are a clever little strandlooper,' Lara told her. 'Let's all go strandlooping after dinner, Mum. I bet I can find some treasures too!'

Mum found an old green bottle, and Lara found a little brown glass jar which they were thrilled with, and Lizzie found some more treasures to add to her collection—a sea urchin shell, unhusked by the sea, and a piece of driftwood that looked like a goanna. By the time they got back to the tent it was nearly dark. Mum lit the gas lamps and built up the fire. Lara made hot chocolate with marshmallows, and she and Mum sang 'Botany Bay' and 'The Lime Juice Tub', 'The North Wind' and 'The Colours of Christmas' but their voices sounded thin and high without Dad's deeper voice beneath them, and after a few songs everyone decided to go to sleep, rather than sit up with their memories under the stars.

All the same, Lara did not feel unhappy as she snuggled down inside her sleeping-bag, and in the night Lizzie only woke once to say 'Daddy!'

Magpies woke Lara next morning, long before the sun was up over the land. She crawled out of the tent and went to look for her mother, whom she found a little way inland among

A Dolphin Dream — Gillian Rubinstein

the dunes, under a small tree. Two magpies were sitting above her, and from where Lara stood they looked as if they were talking to each other.

'What did the magpies say to you?' she asked curiously as the two of them walked back to the tent together.

Mum laughed. She had her country face on, quite different from her city one, and she looked as though someone had been sweeping out her spirit overnight. 'It's funny,' she said, 'but I just love magpies. I feel as though they are my sisters. And, do you know, I have never, ever been attacked by one.'

'If you were a Nungga they would be your totem,' Lara said. She had learned about this at school.

'That's exactly what I think,' Mum replied. 'And when we are out here the land speaks to me so clearly, I could sit and listen to it forever.'

Lara stopped and listened to the land. She could feel it stretching and changing as the sun warmed it. She could hear its myriad animal and plant voices, underpinned by the constant murmur of the sea, and by something else that spoke directly to her own spirit, that told her she was its child.

'Oh, I can hear it too,' she cried, and she and Mum hugged each other.

Lizzie had come out to see where they were, and was staring at them almost jealously.

'Someone else is here!' she announced.

'Here?' Mum repeated in surprise, but what Lizzie meant was another family had set up camp in the night about 500 metres along the beach. A four-wheel drive vehicle was parked on the sand, with two bright coloured tents already erected behind it, and a trailer with a boat and outboard engine alongside it.

'I don't like them,' Lizzie said crossly. 'This is our own private place.'

A Dolphin Dream • Gillian Rubinstein

Lara felt the same, but Mum sighed and said, 'They've got as much right to be here as we have.'

Later they were glad the other camp was there, for none of them was able to open the bottle of gherkins to have with lunch. Lara and Lizzie walked along the beach with the bottle, and the father of the family took it in his brown strong hands and turned the lid as easily as turning on a tap.

'There you go, love,' he said to Lara, handing the bottle back to her. 'No worries. You like fish? You come up in the morning, I'll have some fresh snapper or whiting, with luck.'

There were two boys, Chris, who looked about the same age as Lara, and Alex who was a little bit younger than Lizzie. They both had black hair and golden brown skin, and they wore brightly coloured board shorts. Chris was so thin his board shorts were in danger of falling down altogether, but Alex had a little roll of puppy fat above his, and his legs were chubby. They were very friendly, and after giving the girls a can of coke and showing them their camp and their boat, they walked back with them to say hello to Mum.

Later the children swam together; at least, Chris and Lara swam while Alex jumped up and down on the edge, and Lizzie stayed far up by the high-water mark.

'Come in, Alex!' his brother called to him, but the little boy shook his head, and when Chris went back to lead him in, Alex cried and struggled.

'He's frightened of the sea,' Chris explained to Lara. 'He thinks there are sharks.'

'My sister thinks there are crabs!' Lara said, and then she wanted to stand up for Lizzie, so she added, 'But it's only because she's little.'

A Dolphin Dream • Gillian Rubinstein

'I was never frightened of sharks or crabs even when I was little,' Chris said rather disgustedly. 'Alex is a sook about everything! He's a dead loss!'

By the end of the day Lara agreed thoroughly with this remark and she had almost decided Lizzie was a dead loss too. Alex cried about everything, and Lizzie got in rages. Finally Lara and Chris left them to it, and ran down to have an evening swim when the tide was at its fullest.

After the blazing day the sun was setting into a purple sea and turning the sky the colour of rockmelon. The water where they swam was dark, almost purple too, paling to green above the reef.

'Look!' Chris exclaimed, seizing Lara's arm. 'Dolphins!'

She gazed entranced as the sleek black bodies surfaced through the water. They were close enough for the children to see their clever merry eyes and their hard grey beaks.

The magic of the moment was broken by screams from the shore. Lara and Chris stared in astonishment as Alex came running through the dunes, pursued by a furious Lizzie. Mum appeared from behind the tent, and captured Lizzie as she dashed by. Alex went on running doggedly towards his own tent, and as he ran he scattered something behind him.

'Oh no!' Lara said. 'I think he's got her treasures!' Taking a last reluctant look at the dolphins she galloped out of the water, and Chris followed her.

Lizzie was shrieking hysterically in Mum's arms. 'He stole my things,' she yelled. 'I showed him my treasures and he ran away with them.'

'I'll get them back,' Chris promised. 'Don't cry. I'll make him give them back.'

But Alex had scattered the treasures all over the sand and, though they found the driftwood goanna and the sea urchin

A Dolphin Dream • Gillian Rubinstein

shell, and a lot of shells that might have been Lizzie's, search as they might they could not find the strange bone.

'It was my favourite,' Lizzie said forlornly. 'It was the best treasure I ever found.'

Chris made Alex come back and say he was sorry, and Mum got out lemonade and chips for everyone while she boiled up the water for spaghetti. The dolphins came back and swam up and down through the darkening sea, but even they did not cheer Lizzie up.

Lara went to see if she could help Mum, and found her staring at the sea while the water bubbled and boiled onto the gas stove.

'I was looking at the dolphins,' Mum said, rescuing the spaghetti, 'and remembering how much Dad loved them. Sometimes I feel as if he's just gone for a walk down the beach, and when he comes back I can tell him about them.'

❧

In the middle of the night Lara woke up. The moon was bright on her face through the tent door, and the sleeping-bag next to her was empty. She struggled out of her own bag, hot and thirsty, and went to get a drink of water from the icebox. As she was drinking, she saw a shadowy shape on the beach, halfway between the dunes and the sea.

'Lizzie?' she whispered, going towards it. Lizzie was walking to and fro, her eyes fixed on the sand.

'What are you doing out of bed?' Lara said gently, taking hold of her arm carefully, in case she was sleepwalking. But Lizzie was wide awake. 'I'm looking for my bone,' she said in a normal voice, making Lara jump. 'I woke up and I couldn't get back to sleep and I thought I'd be able to find it 'cause the moon's so bright.'

A Dolphin Dream — Gillian Rubinstein

'I'll look too!' Lara said. The beach at night was beautifully mysterious, with black shadows on the white sand, and the brilliant moon above. The waves hissed gently onto the shore, and the endless sea stretched away into the night. Out towards the horizon little lights showed people were fishing from boats. Chris and his dad were probably out there somewhere, Lara thought, and she wondered if the dolphins were there too.

They searched the sand for a long time but they could not find the bone. Lara wanted to give up, but Lizzie grew more and more stubborn. Finally Lara suggested, more in desperation than anything else, 'Let's sit down for a bit and listen to the spirit of the land. Perhaps it'll tell us where the bone went to.'

Perhaps Lizzie was tired too; anyway, to Lara's relief she sad down rather grumpily on the dry sand above the high-water mark. Lara sat down next to her. 'Put your head on my shoulder and close your eyes,' she said.

After a few moments Lizzie said sleepily, 'I can't hear anything,' and yawned.

'Listen a bit harder,' Lara said, her eyes closed too, and then they suddenly both heard something at the same time, and they opened their eyes with a start.

Out in the sea, something was splashing. They could see the white spray against the black water.

'It must be the dolphins,' Lara said softly. 'Look, Lizzie, aren't they magic!'

The dark shapes glistened as they caught the moonlight. They were coming closer and closer to the shore.

Lizzie said incredulously, 'They're carrying something!'

Between them the dolphins were shouldering a fragile helpless burden, a figure that floated in the water, limbs trailing. The dolphins held up its head with their strong beaks and

A Dolphin Dream • Gillian Rubinstein

nudged it through the shallows until it lay on the sand, nose and mouth free of water, able to breathe air again.

'It's a man!' Lara exclaimed, and made to get up, but at that moment the scene faded, and they could see nothing. At first Lara thought the moon had gone behind a cloud, but then she remembered that the night was cloudless and she realised that they were seeing something that had happened a long, long time ago.

When the darkness cleared and they could see again, the man was standing upright on the beach, facing out to sea. He was a wonderful looking man, like a god or a hero, Lara said later to her mother, with rippling, shining black skin, and thick black hair that curled around his head and glistened under the moon like the dolphins. When he turned to face the land, the children could see his broad nose, and his huge, dark, deep set eyes. His body was painted with glowing white marks and he wore decorations of shells around his neck and limbs.

As they watched he began to dance. He danced swimming far out at sea, and then he danced himself drowning and the dolphins rescuing him. He danced the dolphins bringing him into land, so accurately that the girls had to blink their eyes once or twice to check they were not seeing a dolphin dancing a man. Then the man raced towards the water, and dived into the sea and the dolphins came and danced with him in the shallows until darkness fell again.

Lizzie shivered and Lara sighed deeply, but neither girl could move away. They peered expectantly through the dark, waiting to see what happened next.

When they could see again they both cried out. A dolphin lay stranded on the beach, and the man sat on his heels next to it, wailing with grief.

'Oh, the poor dolphin!' Lara wailed, and Lizzie said urgently, 'What's happened to it? What's happened to it?'

A Dolphin Dream • Gillian Rubinstein

'The dolphin is dead!' Lara said, and next to her Lizzie sobbed quietly, 'The dolphin is dead!'

Then they both hid their faces and cried fresh tears like spring water and, when they looked again, the man was sitting a few metres away from them, singing a low chant and holding something in his hand, something that hung around his neck on a string.

'Don't be afraid,' Lara whispered to Lizzie. 'I don't think he can see us.'

'I'm not afraid of him,' Lizzie replied simply. 'He's a dolphin man and, look, he's wearing my bone!'

Still chanting the dolphin man rose and, stooping low, drew in the clean sea-washed sand. He drew the shape of a dolphin, and then he took the bone from his neck and placed it at a certain point in its tail. Then he sang a high-pitched clicking song, and danced his dolphin dance around the bone.

A splash in the shallows told the children the dolphins were there, watching.

Everything faded, and when the moon returned Lizzie's bone lay a few metres away from them in the sand.

'There it is!' Lara said in surprise. 'However did we miss it before.'

'The dolphin man brought it back,' Lizzie said sleepily. She picked it up and as they staggered off to the tent and their sleeping-bags she was clutching it firmly in her hand.

'Do you think it was a dream?' Lara asked Mum the next morning.

Mum smiled at her. There were tears in her eyes, but they were not really sad ones.

A Dolphin Dream • Gillian Rubinstein

'You can cry, Mum!' Lizzie said generously, giving her a tissue. 'But don't worry abut Dad. He's like the dolphin man. He's dead, but he's still somewhere. Here, or somewhere else. Let's go swimming now.'

'Here come Alex and Chris,' Lara said. 'I expect they've brought us some fish.'

'You can come swimming with me, Alex,' Lizzie announced. 'I won't let anything get you. The dolphins look after me, 'cause I'm a dolphin girl!'

'What about the crabs?' Chris asked, teasingly.

'The crabs are just getting on with living, just like us,' Lizzie said.

For the rest of the holiday they swam and explored the dunes with Chris and Alex, went out in their boat and went strandlooping along the shore. Every day the dolphins in the bay watched them. When it was time to go home, Lizzie grew quieter and quieter as they packed up the camp.

'Are you all right, darling?' Mum asked anxiously. 'I suppose you don't want to leave.'

Lizzie nodded and smiled, but she said nothing until they were in the car, and halfway down the dirt track leading away from the beach. Then she said in a sudden, small voice, 'Mum, do you mind going back?'

'Whatever for?' Mum said in surprise.

'Well, I've got a horrible feeling about taking my bone away. I think it wants to stay here.'

Mum stopped the car, very patiently turned it round and drove slowly back to their camp site.

'Why does it want to stay here?' Lara questioned.

A Dolphin Dream — Gillian Rubinstein

'This is where it belongs. This is where its dreams happen,' Lizzie replied slowly.

Where its dreams happen, Lara repeated to herself. As she followed Lizzie across the sand, still wet from last night's tide, she undid the clasp of her father's necklace.

They stopped at a point halfway between the dunes and the sea, and Lizzie dug a hole and buried the bone. Then Lara dug a hole a little way from it and buried the necklace.

When they got to their feet, they saw the dolphins leap and dive through the turquoise water.

Both home now, Lara said to herself. Both dolphin men have come home.

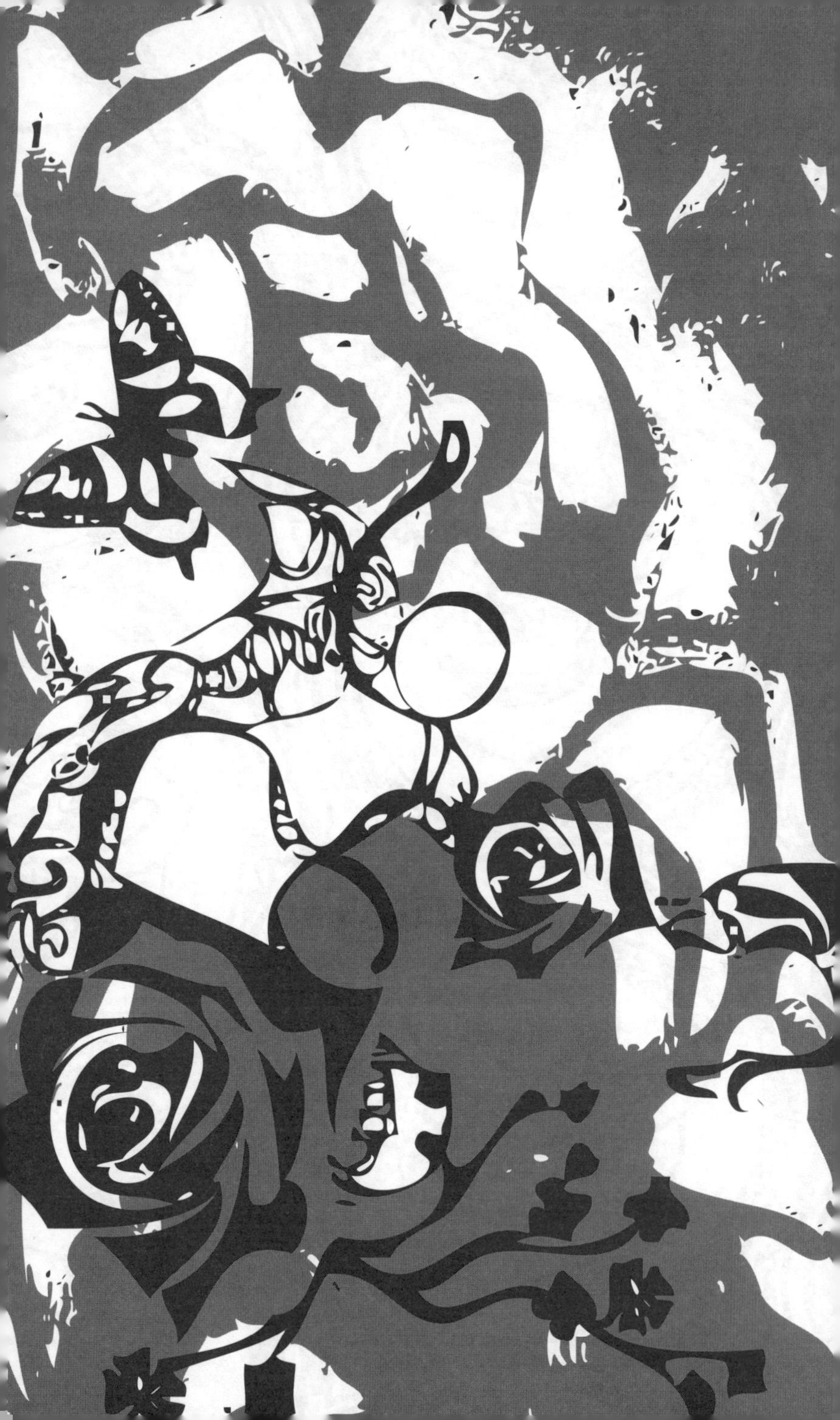

THREE ROSES

Garth Nix

Three Roses — Garth Nix

THIS is the story of a gardener who grew the most beautiful single rose the world had ever seen. It was a black rose, which was unlikely, and it bloomed the whole year round, which was impossible.

Hearing of this rose, the King decided to see it for himself. With his entourage, he rode for seven days to the gardener's simple cottage. On the morning of the seventh day, he arrived and saw the rose. It was even more beautiful than the King had imagined, and he wanted it.

'How did you come to grow such a beautiful rose?' the King asked the gardener, who was standing silently by.

'I planted that rose on the day my wife died,' replied the gardener, looking only at the flower. 'It is a true, deep black, the very colour of her hair. The rose grew from my love of her.'

The King turned to his servants and said, 'Uproot this rosebush and take it to the palace. It is too beautiful for anyone but me.'

But when the rosebush was transplanted to the palace, it lasted only a year before it withered and died. The King, who had gazed upon it every day, angrily decided that it was the gardener's fault, and he set out at once to punish him.

But when he arrived at the gardener's cottage, he was amazed to see a new rosebush growing there, with a single rose. But this rose was green, and even more beautiful than the black rose.

The King once again asked the gardener how he came to grow such a beautiful rose.

'I planted this rose on the anniversary of my wife's death,' said the gardener, his eyes only on the rose. 'It is the colour of her eyes, which I looked into every morning. The rose grew from my love of her.'

Three Roses — Garth Nix

'Take it!' commanded the King, and he turned away to ride the seven days back to his palace. Such a beautiful flower was not fit for a common man.

The green rose bloomed for two years, and the King looked upon it every day, for it brought him great contentment. Then, one morning, it was dead, the bush withered, the petals fallen to the ground. The King picked up the petals and spoke to no one for two days. Then he said, as if to convince himself, 'The gardener will have another rose.'

So once again he rode off with his entourage. This time, they took a spade and the palace jardinier.

Such was the King's impatience that they rode for half the nights as well as days, but there were wrong turns and flooded bridges, and it still took seven days before he once again rode up to the gardener's cottage. And there was a new rosebush, with a single rose. A red rose, so beautiful that the King's men were struck silent and the King himself could only stare and gesture to the palace jardinier to take it away.

Even though the King didn't ask, the gardener spoke before the spade broke the earth around the bush.

'I planted this rose three years after the death of my wife,' he said. 'It is the colour of her lips, which I first kissed under a harvest moon on the hottest of summer nights. This rose grew from my love of her.'

The King seemed not to hear but kept staring at the rose. Finally, he tore his gaze away and turned his horse for home.

The jardinier watched him go and stopped digging for a moment.

'Your roses are the most beautiful I have ever seen,' he said. 'They could only grow from a great love. But why grow them only to have these memories taken from you?'

The gardener smiled and said, 'I need nothing to remind me of my wife. When I walk alone under the night sky, I see the blackness of her hair. When the light catches the green glass of a bottle, I see her eyes. When the sun is setting all red against the hills and the wind touches my cheek, I feel her kiss.

'I grew the first rose because I was afraid I might forget. When it was gone, I knew that I had lost nothing. No one can take the memory of my love.'

The jardinier frowned, and he began to cut again with his spade. Then he asked, 'But why do you keep growing the roses?'

'I grow them for the King,' said the gardener. 'He has no memories of his own, no love. And after all, they are only flowers.'

Round the Bend

Paul Jennings

Round the Bend – Paul Jennings

*T*HUMP.

'Oh, gawd,' said my friend Derek.

'What?'

'We've run over a dog.'

Derek's dad looked in the mirror and pulled the Mercedes over to the side of the road. The three of us jumped out and started walking back to the small, still bundle in the middle of the road.

'Don't worry,' said Derek. 'My dad will take care of things.'

We were on our way to a volleyball game. Derek's dad was taking a shortcut because we were late.

It was dark and hard to see. But the dog seemed to be lying very still. I didn't want to look. What if it was dead and all squashed, with blood and guts hanging out? Or even worse—what if it was squashed and alive? What would we do then?

I could feel my stomach churning. I rushed over to a bush and threw up. The spew splashed all over my shoes. Ugh. I hate being sick. And I hate looking like a wimp.

Derek's dad had already reached the dog. He was bending down, trying to see in the dark. Before he could move, a feeble voice filtered through the trees. 'Tinker, Tinker. Come here, boy. Where are you?'

A little old man with wispy hair stumbled onto the road. 'Have you seen—' he started to say. His gaze fell on the small dog lying on the road. 'Tinker?' he said. He fell to his knees with a sob and started to feel all over the dog. He tried to find a pulse.

Round the Bend • Paul Jennings

'Gone,' he said looking up at us as if we were murderers. 'Our poor little Tinker.'

We all stared guiltily at each other. I didn't know what to say. Derek and I walked over to the dog. It was very dark but I could see a little smear of blood coming out of one nostril. The dog was a bit flat and stiff. But that was all. No bones sticking out or anything awful like that. If it wasn't for the glassy, staring eyes you might have thought it was still alive.

The old man clasped the dog to his chest as if it was a baby. Then he stumbled off towards a nearby farmhouse without another word.

I wanted to get back in the car and drive off. I just wanted to put a big distance between us and what we had done. But not Derek's dad. He was so calm. He always knew what to do. He was a pilot in the airforce. He flew Phantom jets. Once he had to bail out over Bass Strait when an engine caught fire. He was a hero. Strong and handsome and tough.

Just the opposite of my dad. Don't get me wrong. I love my dad. But ... well, let's face it. He's no oil painting. And he drives a beat-up old truck. And he's not a pilot. He's a ...

I just couldn't bring myself to say it. Derek was always asking me what my dad does. I didn't want to tell him. It was too awful.

Derek's dad stared up the track. What was he going to do? Jump in the car and drive off? No way. 'Listen, boys,' he said. 'We have to do the right thing. We have to try and make up for what we've done.'

'Dad always does the right thing,' said Derek proudly.

A light was shining on the porch of the small farmhouse. Derek's dad started to walk towards it. We followed along behind. I had a sinking feeling in my stomach. And it wasn't because I'd just been sick.

Round the Bend • Paul Jennings

The old man might not be very pleased to see us. He might go troppo.

But then I cheered up. After all, Derek's dad had parachuted out of a jet fighter at ten thousand metres. He could handle anything.

❧

Derek's dad knocked on the farmhouse door. Not a little timid knock like my dad would have done. A real loud, confident knock. Derek smiled.

There was a bit of shuffling and rustling inside and then the door swung open. I could just make out the shape of the dog covered by a blanket in front of the fire inside. The old man stared at us with tear-filled eyes. His lips started to tremble. For a minute I thought he was going to faint.

'The dog just ran out of nowhere,' said Derek's dad. 'We didn't even see it.'

'Tinker,' said the old man. 'Poor darling Tinker.'

'We'd like to do something,' said Derek's dad. 'I know how you must feel.'

The old man beckoned us inside. Derek's dad gave us a confident nod and led the way. The room was gloomy, lit only by a lamp. The old man collapsed into a chair and sank his head into his hands. He started to sob and rub at his eyes. Then he looked up and spoke.

'Please excuse me,' he said. 'I'm not crying for me. I'm crying for Jason.'

'Jason?' said Derek's dad.

The old man held a finger to his lips. Then he hobbled across the room and silently opened a door. We tiptoed over and peeped in. A small boy with a pale face was sleeping peacefully in a rough wooden bed.

Round the Bend • Paul Jennings

'My grandson, Jason,' said the old man. 'His parents were both killed in a car accident last year. He wouldn't talk to anyone. Not a word. Just sat looking at the wall. Until I bought him that dog. As a puppy. It got him talking again. "Tinker," he said. "I'll call him Tinker." '

A tear started to run down the old man's cheek.

We all fell silent and stared at Jason lying there asleep. The poor kid. His parents were dead. And now his dog, Tinker, was dead too. What would he say when he woke up? Would he lose his speech again?

Derek's dad pulled out his wallet. 'I'll pay for a new dog,' he said.

'Good on ya, Dad,' said Derek. His dad was so kind. He couldn't bring Tinker back to life but he was going to pay for a replacement. We all stared at the wallet. It was stuffed full of money. That was another good thing about Derek's dad. He was rich.

The old man shook his head. 'He won't take to a new dog,' he said. 'It'll have to be Tinker or nothing.'

Derek's dad shook his head sadly. 'I can't bring Tinker back from the dead,' he said. 'No one can do that. But where did you get the dog?'

The old man brightened up a bit. 'Fish Creek,' he said. 'There's a guy down there who breeds them.'

We spent ages driving around country back roads. In the middle of the night. Looking for the kennels at Fish Creek where the dead dog came from. 'We'll never find it,' I groaned.

Derek's dad stopped the car at a dark crossroads. 'Get out, boys,' he said.

We scrambled out of the car and stood there in the silent countryside. Derek and I didn't have a clue what was going on.

Round the Bend • Paul Jennings

'Listen,' said Derek's dad.

We listened. We strained our ears. Nothing but crickets and frogs. But then. Then. Faintly. Far away. The sound of dogs barking. We all grinned. Derek's dad was so smart.

'You're a genius, Dad,' said Derek.

I thought about my own dad. He would be at the volleyball match. He'd gone on ahead. On his own. He knew I wanted to have a ride in the Mercedes. He didn't mind having no one to talk to. My dad was a quiet person.

Derek's dad followed the sound of the dogs until we came to the kennels. It was a ratty old place with cages and dumped cars everywhere. As we drew up to the house dozens of dogs began to snarl and snap and howl. I was glad they were in cages. They sounded like they wanted to tear us to pieces.

A big guy in a blue singlet staggered out and looked into the car. He had a bushy beard. In one hand he held a stubby of beer. Over on the porch I saw a speedboat. A brand-new one by the look of it.

'Nick off,' growled the guy in the blue singlet. 'We don't like strangers in the middle of the night.'

Derek's dad opened his wallet. 'We've come to buy a dog,' he said.

'Yeah,' said Derek.

The bloke grinned with big yellow teeth and opened the car door. 'In that case,' he said. 'Come in.'

Derek's dad told him the story of little Jason and the dead dog and how we wanted another one the same before he woke up.

'Only one left from the litter,' said the dog breeder. 'And I can't remember if it looks the same as Tinker.' He led us out to a shed and showed us a dog. We all smiled at each other. It

Round the Bend ⋅ Paul Jennings

was exactly the same as the dead dog. It even had a little brown patch on its left ear.

'Just the shot,' beamed Derek's dad. 'How much?'

'A thousand dollars.'

Derek's dad turned pale. 'How much?' he said again.

'A thousand bucks,' said the dog breeder. 'This is my breeding bitch. It's the only female in the country. They are very rare dogs. Mongolian Rat Catchers.'

'You can afford it, Dad,' said Derek. 'Go on, buy it.'

Derek's dad looked at us. He looked at the dog breeder. He looked at the dog. Then he handed over the thousand dollars. In cash.

What a man. Fancy paying a thousand dollars. Just to help out a little boy he didn't even know.

'My father doesn't even have a thousand dollars,' I thought to myself. 'Geez, Derek is lucky.'

'Let's go,' said Derek's dad. 'We have to get back with this dog before little Jason wakes up and finds out that Tinker is dead.'

We jumped into the Mercedes and tore back to the farmhouse. The little man opened the door before we could even knock. 'He's still asleep,' he whispered. 'Come in quick.'

We all walked into the gloomy room and Derek's dad put the new dog on the table. It immediately started to lick the little man's hand. He peered at it carefully and then wiped tears of joy from his eyes. 'Amazing,' he said. 'It's exactly the same. Jason will never know the difference.'

The new dog wagged its tail happily.

'Where's the dead dog?' asked Derek's dad.

Round the Bend ❧ Paul Jennings

The little man picked up a sack and opened it. We all stared into the gloom at the dead dog. There was no doubt about it. You just couldn't tell the difference between the two animals.

The new dog jumped off the table, ran over to the sack and started barking like crazy. It didn't like what was in there at all. The noise was enough to wake the dead. 'Tinker, Tinker?' came a boy's weak voice. The old man threw a quick look at little Jason's door and quickly pushed the sack aside. Then he grabbed the new dog and took it into the bedroom.

We all followed him into the room. Jason was sitting up in bed, calling to the new dog feebly. He looked at it. He frowned. He looked puzzled. 'Tinker,' he said in a worried voice. 'You've lost your collar.'

The old man shuffled back into the kitchen, put his hand into the sack and took the collar from the dead dog. 'Here it is,' he said. 'I was just cleaning it.'

Jason threw out his arms and hugged the new dog. 'Oh Tinker,' he said. 'I love you.'

❧

The Mercedes wound its way through the mountains. Now we were really late for the volleyball match. 'It was worth a thousand dollars,' said Derek's dad. 'Just to see the look on that poor boy's face.' Derek and I smiled at each other. What a man he was. Always so calm.

'You're the greatest, Dad,' said Derek. He looked at me to see if I was going to disagree. I didn't.

When we got to the volleyball stadium my own dad was not calm.

'Where have you been?' he growled. 'The game's over. I thought you must have been in an accident. I was just about to call the police.'

Round the Bend • Paul Jennings

'Calm down, old boy,' said Derek's dad. 'We've got quite a story to tell you.'

Dad listened to the whole thing in silence. He didn't seem impressed.

'Mongolian Rat Catcher,' he said grumpily. 'Never heard of them.'

'Know about dogs, do you?' said Derek's dad. 'Work with animals, do you?'

Dad looked annoyed. He opened his mouth to tell them what he does but I got in first. 'Er, we'd better be going,' I said.

Dad drove back down the mountain. Fast. He asked me a lot of questions about Jason and the dog breeder and the old man. But he didn't say much. He was in a grumpy mood. Why couldn't he be cool? Like Derek's dad.

'It's up here,' I said. 'The place where we hit the dog. Just round the bend.'

Dad dropped down a gear and planted his foot. He roared round the corner really fast. Boy, he was in a bad mood.

THUMP.

'Aaagh,' I screamed.

'What?'

'We've run over a dog.'

Dad looked in the mirror and pulled the truck over to the side of the road. The two of us jumped out and started walking back to the small, still bundle in the middle of the road.

My heart jumped up into my mouth. I felt faint. I felt sick. Dad had run over Jason's new dog. And killed it. I just couldn't believe it. The same thing had happened. Twice. In the same night. But now it was Dad who had killed the dog.

And there was no way he was going to be able to fix things up. He didn't have a thousand dollars. And anyway, there were no more Mongolian Rat Catchers left. We couldn't pull the same trick again.

Dad bent over and looked at the dead dog carefully.

Before he could move, a trembling voice filtered through the trees. 'Tinker, Tinker. Come here, boy. Where are you?'

The little old man with the wispy hair stumbled onto the road. 'Have you seen—' he started to say. His gaze fell on the small dog lying on the road. 'Tinker?' He said. He fell to his knees with a sob and started to feel all over the dog. His fingers felt for a pulse.

'Gone,' he said looking up at us as if we were murderers. Then his eyes opened wide as he recognised me. 'You've killed two dogs in the same night,' he gasped.

The old man clasped the dog to his chest as if it was a baby. Then he stumbled off towards the nearby farmhouse without another word. Just like he'd done before.

'Hey,' shouted Dad. 'Come back here.'

Why couldn't my dad be more kind and generous? Like Derek's dad. My dad didn't even seem sorry for what he had done. The little man stopped and Dad went towards him.

'Go back to the truck,' Dad growled at me.

I did. I was glad to go back to the truck. I didn't want to see that look in the old man's eyes. I didn't want to hear Jason start crying when he saw the dead dog.

After about ten minutes Dad came back to the truck. He had the dead dog with him. He threw the body onto the back of the truck and started up the engine. 'Show me how to get to the dog kennels,' he said.

'It's no good,' I yelled. 'There are no more Mongolian Rat Catchers left. It was the last one.'

'Just show me the way,' said Dad.

Round the Bend • Paul Jennings

We drove in silence. Except for when I had to point out which way to turn. Why wouldn't Dad listen to me? Why did he have to go back to the dog breeder's place? It was crazy.

Finally, we reached the dog kennels. The dogs started up howling and barking just like before. Dad didn't even wait for the dog breeder to come out. He jumped out of the truck and ran up to the door. I saw it open and Dad disappeared inside.

There was a lot of yelling and shouting. What was going on? Should I go and help? Just then the door flew open and Dad came out. He angrily shoved his wallet into his pocket and strode across to our old truck.

Dad didn't have a new dog for little Jason. He didn't even have the dead dog. He was dogless. And he wasn't in the mood for talking.

Neither was I. Why couldn't my dad be calm and cool and rich? Why couldn't my dad have a wallet full of money to buy a new dog for Jason? Why did we have to drive around in a beat-up old truck and not a Mercedes? Why, why, why?

After a long drive we got back to town. Dad stopped outside the front gate.

Of Derek's house.

'What are we doing here?' I said. 'They're probably in bed.'

Dad gave me a big smile. He ruffled my hair in a friendly way. 'Come on, Ned,' he said. 'I don't think they'll mind.'

Derek's dad threw open the front door and stared at us. So did Derek.

'Hello, old boy,' said Derek's dad. 'What's up?'

Dad took out his wallet.

'Oh, no,' I thought. 'He's going to ask Derek's dad for money.'

But he didn't. Dad took out a great wad of notes. 'Here's your thousand dollars back,' he said.

I stared. Derek stared. We all stared.

Dad smiled. 'Tinker was dead all right,' he said. 'A stuffed dead dog. With glass eyes. The little man threw it under every car that passed. Then he sent the guilty driver off to buy the other dog. That dog breeder has sold his Mongolian Rat Catcher to at least fifty suckers.'

Derek's dad took his money back and stood there with his jaw hanging open. 'How did you know?' he stammered.

I looked at Derek and decided to answer the question myself. I was so happy.

'He's a taxidermist,' I said proudly.

SNAKE MAN

Sophie Masson

O NCE upon a time, in a village snoozing by the side of a blue African lake, lived a young girl and her father, the chief. The place where they lived was beautiful. There was lush grass for cattle, and wild game in plenty. At night, elephants and hippos, rhinos and zebra, lion and impala would come down to drink at the lake. The chief's hut was decorated with red and yellow and black paintings, and the thatch of it was soft and strong.

The girl's mother had died many years ago, and the chief doted on his only child, giving her everything her heart desired. She had more beautiful cloths to wind around herself, more costly bead jewellery than any other chief's daughter for miles around. She would often watch herself in the mirror of the lake, and sigh, for she knew she was beautiful.

When the time came for the girl to marry, the chief summoned all the young men from near and far. They came from the village and from the settlements beyond, fine handsome young men in costly finery, with eyes full of love. But the girl turned up her nose at all of them, and sent them away with a disdainful air. She laughed at this one's small eyes, this one's big teeth, this one's silly beard, till they went away, heads hung in shame, their presents of bananas and meat flung into the lake.

The girl's father was not pleased, but once again he summoned young men, this time from the kingdom beyond the hills, and from the chiefdom by the great river. Strong young men they were, too, with hair plaited and strengthened with red mud, blue and green and gold jewellery about their necks. Their spears rattled as they declared their love for the chief's daughter, but she remained unmoved, her mouth drawn down in anger.

'Noisy like chickens!' she said as she dismissed them.

Her father was angry now, but still he sent for more suitors. They came, still they came, from the mountains many miles beyond, from the shores of the far-distant sea. A great crowd of them there were: upstanding young men in leopard skins and cloth of gold, in rustling bright cloths and turbans, in plaited straw and some with painted bodies. But the chief's daughter folded her arms and looked out beyond them, at the sun setting on the lake, and said not a word.

'Daughter,' said her father, 'you must decide which of these men is to be your husband.' But his daughter shook her head.

'I will have none of these, none of these! I want a prince of renown, not these overgrown boys. Tell them to return to their distant lands!'

The chief was in a rage. He pleaded and threatened, but to no avail. All the young men were sent home again, and the girl returned to her quiet life by the lake, dreaming of a handsome prince and a life of ease.

A few days later she was sitting by the side of the lake as usual, watching her reflection in the blue still water, when at her elbow appeared a beautiful young man. She had not heard him approach, so silently had he come on soft feet.

Straightaway the girl's foolish heart went out to him, for was he not strong and bright like a prince? His eyes were dark brown, his skin as shining as copper, his arms weighted down with gold, and—strange to relate—his tongue was pink and darting and honeyed from behind lips as ripe as a mango.

He spoke softly to the girl, and her heart was taken, so she took him to her father's hut to tell him this would be her promised one.

Her father was pleased, for the new suitor gave him many costly presents of gold and ivory, and drove many more fine cattle into his Kraal.

Snake Man • Sophie Masson

So the wedding feast was held, and such a feast it was, lasting for three days and nights. The maize beer flowed aplenty, goats were slaughtered, and the young men of the village sang songs of praise—all but one, who had loved the chief's daughter since they were children together. This young man was sad and uneasy, for no one in the whole village had ever heard of the new bridegroom or of the village he said he came from.

The hour came when the bridegroom announced that he was taking his new wife to his people's village, far beyond the lake, in the depths of the forest.

'It is not far,' he said to the old father, 'not far to visit her.' And the old man, sad at losing his only child, wept silently and nodded his head. But the girl did not weep; she was excited and proud to be setting off with her prince, the love of her heart.

They journeyed far, for a day or more, till they came to a village hidden deep in the forest, and the girl went forward eagerly to greet her new kinsfolk. But horrors! What was this she saw? Instead of warriors and maidens, mothers and fathers, who should come out of the village but a tribe of giant snakes! They slithered around her legs and hissed a sibilant welcome, and when the frightened girl turned to her new husband for help, there was no longer a gay young prince before her, but a huge, slithering, copper-coloured snake with glittering eyes and a darting, pink, honeyed tongue.

The girl screamed and tried to run away, but the snakes chased her and brought her back, and from that day on treated her with great cruelty. She was made to do all the work in the village, fill the pitchers with water, tend the gardens, pound the maize and make the meals. Her snake husband treated her worst of all. She had to lie with him in the bottomless black nights, while his old snake-mother crouched by the fire and sang a snake's hissing song.

And when the deepest of the night arrived, all the snakes left the village to hunt for prey in the depths of the silent forest that surrounded them. They caught rats, mice and creeping things for the girl to prepare for their meal the next day. She had to stay alone in the hut with the old snake-mother, who hissed in her sleep. The girl was very unhappy: how she longed for her blue lake and her village and her father, and how she wished she had not been so haughty and spoilt!

After a time, it happened that the old chief her father fell ill, and he sent a messenger to his son-in-law's village in the forest, and the messenger was none other than the young man who had long loved the chief's daughter from afar.

The young man took his stoutest spear and his greatest courage, and he set off for the village in the forest.

When he arrived late at night, instead of going straight in, he hid himself in the bushes at the entrance of the village.

Soon, from the huts, he saw the snakes emerging, two by two in their brilliant skins, and at the head of them a large, copper-coloured snake with gold bands around his body and a darting, pink tongue.

The young man stiffened in horror at the sight, but he kept silent and watched them pass into the depths of the forest. Then he crept into the silent village. Into one hut after another he peered, until he came to the one where the chief's daughter sat weeping over her pots, yearning for her lost village by the side of the lake. She started when she saw him, and he was about to cry out to her, when he noticed the old snake-mother lying motionless by the fire, hissing in her sleep.

The young man had no trouble persuading the girl to come back with him to her home village, but just as they reached the edge of the snake-village, the old mother woke up and, seeing her prize gone, hissed a terrible sound. All the hunting snakes in the forest heard her cry, and set off in pursuit of the pair.

They came slithering after them, their angry tongues darting, hissing vengeance.

Onwards the young couple ran, onwards, until it seemed they could run no further, and the snakes were gaining on them. Then the young man stopped and broke a branch off a tree, and made fire, so that he had a burning torch, which he hurled at the advancing snakes. The fire roared and threw itself on the snakes, who hissed and tried to escape it. But most of them were caught in the flames and burnt, and in the middle of them the huge copper-coloured snake, the girl's husband. As his body flamed, he hissed at her, 'I will see you again!'

Those of the snakes that escaped made their way back to their village, and were never seen near human settlements again. The young couple went home.

The chief's daughter and the young man were married, and there was much rejoicing in the village. The chief rose from his sickbed and kissed his daughter with tears in his eyes.

But the couple's first child, a fine son, was born with copper skin, and glittering eyes, and a pink, darting little tongue.

Adapted from a Shona folktale

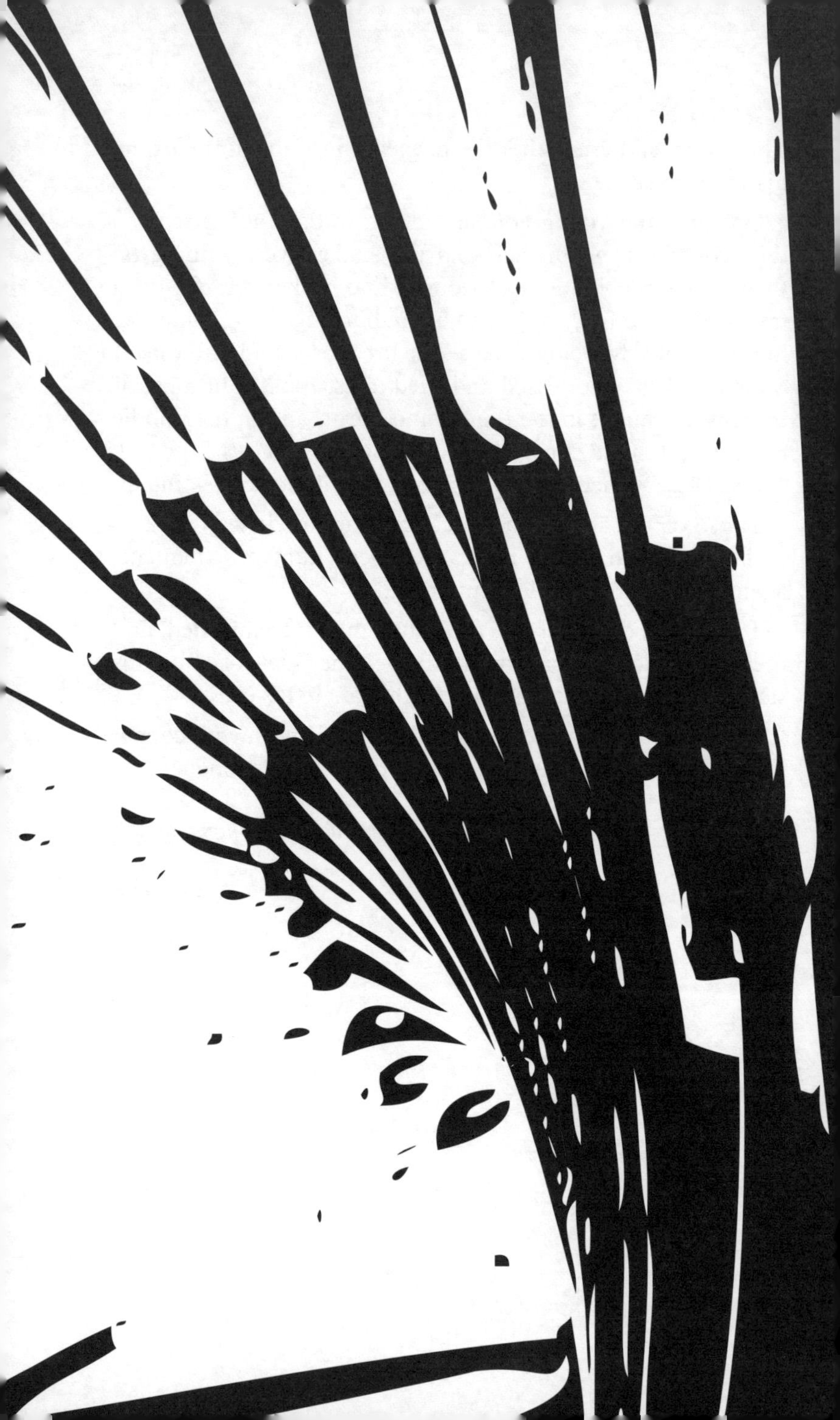

CHEAT!

Allan Baillie

cheat! — Allan Baillie

LYNNE shut her eyes as the headmaster droned on, and shouted at him silently. Shut up, just stop it, shut up so we can go home. Please!

She wanted him to read a name, and by now it didn't matter whose name it was. She just wanted it to finish.

'... we had a long struggle in separating the two top entries in the short story competition,' Mr Velos said.

Lynne opened her eyes and gripped her seat.

It must be her and someone else. It must be her.

'Geoff Bolder and Lynne Webbings both wrote very fine short stories for the medal ...'

Lynne felt her mouth moving, but she was not smiling. Not now. She glanced sideways and Geoff was grinning at her.

'Lynne's story about a sheepdog in a flood was both exciting and moving ...'

Perhaps a tie.

Lynne felt slightly ill. She could remember the hours, the weeks, she had put in over that miserable story. The plotting, the characterisation—how do you create a character from a one-eyed, dumb red kelpie, anyway?—the atmosphere, the tension. The writing, the rewriting, the tearing up of the tale, and starting it over again. Oh, and the pain in pulling it all together.

It had to be a tie.

'... but Geoff's story of a circus elephant running loose in Albert Park we found very funny. Comedy, we know, is harder to write than drama ... Congratulations Geoff, on winning the Holmes–Watkins Medal!'

cheat! — Allan Baillie

Lynne blinked hard, and smiled, and shrugged to her friends and clapped like everyone else.

Ah well, second is not so bad, is it?

She made her way to Geoff as he came down from the dais with the medal and congratulated him. She went home and everything tasted of cardboard that night.

Lynne put her short story aside and walked slowly away from her disappointment. After a while she could even meet Geoff without feeling a quiver of pain. Geoff helped in that.

'Found out how Velos picks the winner,' said Geoff.

'Oh?'

'Climbs on top of his lovely special mahogany desk—almost falls off when the school bell goes off. Anyway he stands on his desk with your story in his right hand and mine in his left, reaches up, tippy-toe, and drops them both. The one that hits the floor first is the winner.'

Lynne laughed.

'Really. Next time use heavier paper.'

And after that Lynne was back to normal. Geoff was all right, even if he'd made it hard to listen to Ol' Velos with a straight face. Her story was abandoned in a drawer as she concentrated on making the school basketball team.

Until she read a book of short stories by the author William Bradburie. And one of Bradburie's stories was of an elephant which escaped in a park, causing hopeless confusion.

She read it again. And again. The tips of her ears prickled with anger.

'The cheat,' she said slowly, meaning the word for the first time in her life. 'He didn't write it at all. He just copied it down.'

She realised that if Velos knew about this he would take the medal from Geoff, and Geoff might have to leave the school.

cheat! Allan Baillie

He would deserve it!

But who would tell Velos?

'I will.' Lynne was talking hollowly in an empty room.

She pictured Velos standing before her. All right, how?

Please sir, Geoff beat me in the short story competition and I hate to lose. So I'm telling you how he cheated so you can give the medal to me.

No. No, that would be terrible. You can't do that.

What about getting a friend to tell him. Marge—she'd do it.

But she wouldn't really like you after that.

Write him an anonymous letter.

You'd be worse than he is.

But he doesn't deserve to win!

He's won. There's nothing you can do about it.

She closed the book and turned away.

The next day the form master, Matheson, was asking the class what careers they had in mind. Marge said she'd like to be a Grand Prix driver but she didn't suppose Mum would allow that so she'd settle for being a surgeon. When the laughter stopped Matheson looked at Geoff.

'Well, here's one boy who should have an idea of where he's going, eh Geoff?'

Geoff looked up blankly.

'What are you interested in, Geoff? TV scriptwriting, screenwriting, playwriting, being an author?'

'Oh, nup. None of that. I am going to be a barrister.'

'A lawyer? I thought with your recent triumph you would have your eye on a different direction.'

'Nah, there's more money in law.'

'I suppose so ... yes, Lynne?'

cheat! Allan Baillie

Lynne suddenly realised she was half-standing in her desk, with her mouth working and Marge staring up at her. 'Sir, I ...' She looked at Geoff who was smiling at her. She sat down heavily. 'I forget, sir.'

Outside, Lynne drifted into a group forming around Geoff. When she became aware of who was talking she tried to shuffle away, but there were too many kids looking at her and she could not appear to be jealous of Geoff. Marge was abusing Geoff for being so devoted to money.

'Why? What's wrong with money?'

'It's dull. Think of the excitement you're missing. You could get on television like Roald Dahl and Paul Jennings.'

'Who wants television anyway?'

'—or Bradburie.' The words exploded from Lynne's mouth in a sudden burst of anger.

Geoff looked at her and frowned.

'Who's Bradburie?' Marge asked.

'Oh, Geoff reads him.'

Geoff started to smile at some joke he did not understand but for a moment his eyes quivered. The bantering conversation went on but he seemed to be drifting away.

Later Lynne saw that all the Bradburie books had been taken from the school library.

He's trying to hide the story he stole his idea from, Lynne thought grimly. It won't do him any good. Sooner or later, sooner or later ...

But five minutes into the next period Velos sent for her.

He's got Velos to stick up for him now. Shut up little girl or you will be in detention until you are a grey-haired old lady. I just won't shut up!

cheat! ▸ Allan Baillie

But Velos was sitting heavily behind his desk, fiddling with a pencil, and he looked embarrassed. The medal was resting on an open Bradburie book near his elbow. Geoff was standing, hunched, off to one side and he was avoiding her eyes.

Velos has caught him! There was no need to get all tied up in knots. Now we'll see …

'Lynne,' Velos said slowly. He seemed to be picking the words as they lay on his tongue. 'I have been talking to Geoff about the medal.'

'Oh.' Lynne carefully kept all feeling from her voice, but Geoff lifted his head, looking at her with pain in his eyes.

'To come to the point. I am telling you this so you can understand. Geoff has told me that three years ago he read a book by the American humorist William Bradburie and he had forgotten about it until today.'

Velos placed the pencil on the desk and looked at Lynne. 'I read the book. There's a story there about an elephant escaping in a park. It is not much like Geoff's story, but Geoff feels he took the idea from the book without realising it. He wants me to disqualify him for cheating.'

'No!' Lynne was appalled. Everything was changing.

'Exactly. Geoff hasn't cheated—his story is almost entirely his own—he has only shown that he has a bad memory. So we won't disqualify him, but I think we must reverse the positions of you two. Your story, Lynne, being entirely original, must be considered a little better than Geoff's. I apologise to you both.'

Geoff caught Lynne as she shambled along the corridor. 'I'm sorry Lynne, really sorry, but it's fixed now.'

Lynne shook her head and forced the words out. 'I didn't want to win that way.'

'I know,' Geoff said. 'But I can't do anything else … Sorry.' He left her and walked tiredly to his class.

cheat! ❧ Allan Baillie

Lynne leaned against a locker and tried to swallow the bitter taste from her mouth.

She began to wonder where it was that she had read a story about a sheepdog in a flood.

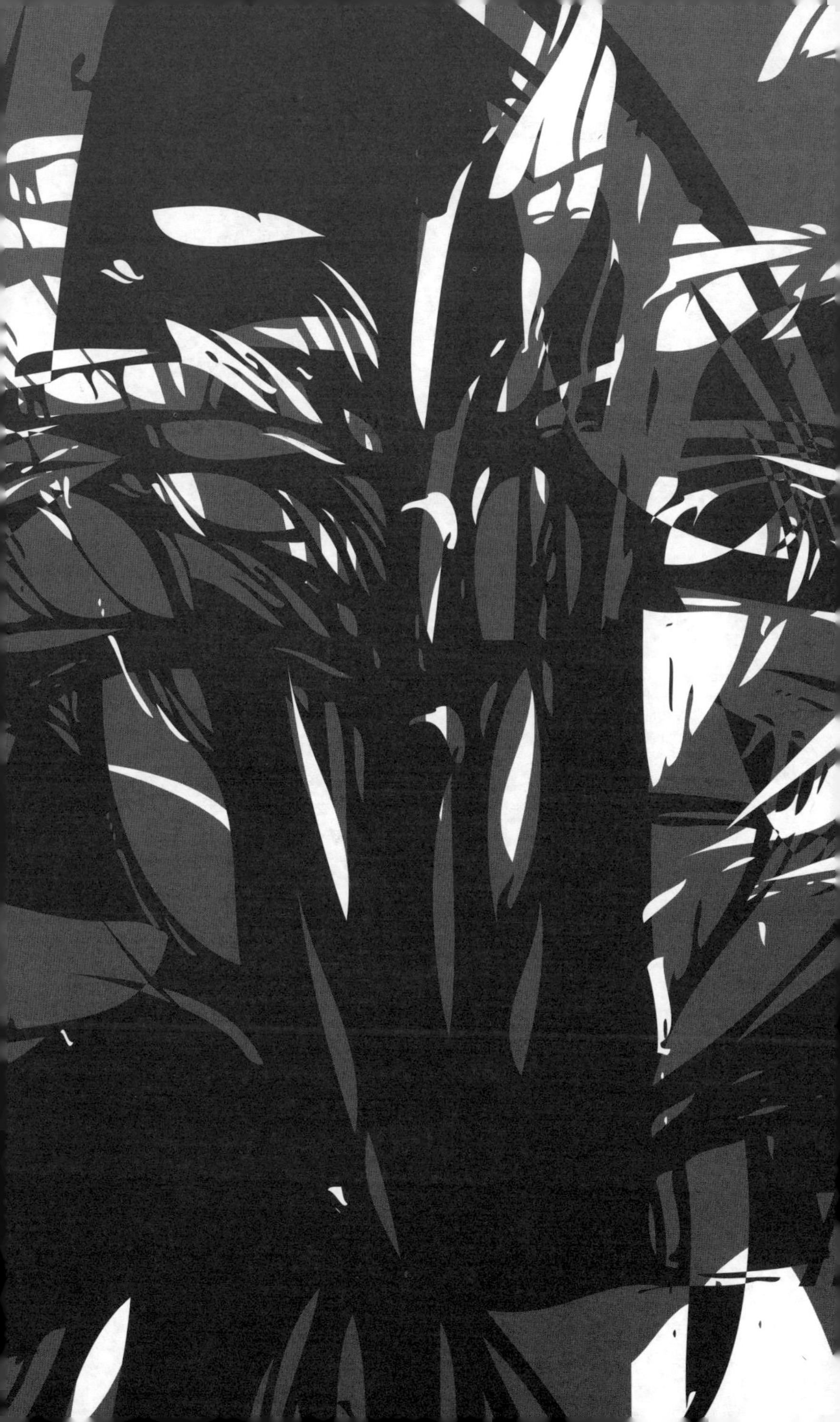

RAIN

Libby Gleeson

Rain ~ Libby Gleeson

RAIN.

It's all they talk about. In class, in the playground.

And I've got nothing to say.

I stare out the window at the great pools of water where the leaves have blocked the drains at the edge of the verandah. I think it will all spread, flooding back into the room, but Joe Brack comes along with his broom just in time and pushes the leaves away. The water gets sucked in like a giant whirlpool.

'... and so,' said Mr Burrows, 'it looks like we may be in for another flood this year.'

That starts them. Flood stories. Cows drowning, chooks drowning, sheep drowning. Wayne Drury says that in the last flood two years ago they had water in their house and all their carpet and lino was rotten and they had to pull it all up and change it when the water went down. It smelt for days.

Amy Chapman reckons that was nothing. They had to move out. Their back shed got washed away and their outside toilet. She says it stank to high heaven for weeks and weeks.

Nina Stevens is next. Her dad is a policeman and he had to go round in the last flood and tell people when they had to get out of their houses and sometimes they wouldn't leave and he had to make them. There were people who said they'd built their houses themselves, they'd had all their kids grow up there and they weren't leaving, not for anyone.

Everyone in the class remembers the last flood.

'And what about you, Katy, I suppose you've never been in a flood?' He says it kindly enough but everyone turns and stares.

I shake my head. A flood in Bondi. As if.

Rain • Libby Gleeson

I think about lying, saying that yes, I have been, that in the last place we lived it always flooded and sometimes we got trapped, bogged just like Michael Donnelly's sheep and Jan Shank's cows and we even had to be rescued in a boat and my dad got abused by a policeman. But I know if I make up a big lie, somehow I'll get something wrong and then I'll get found out and made to look really, really stupid. I know about high tides, huge waves, strong rips. I've even seen the body of a tourist who drowned.

I don't know about floods.

So I say nothing and slip back into my shadow.

It is still raining when the bell goes. I catch the bus to Mum's work. I sit up by the driver and the huge wipers swish across the windscreen, flinging the water back out into the air. When Mum comes out, she points to a line on the wall of the reception area, about where my armpits are.

'That's the marking of the great flood,' she said.

'Noah?'

'Don't be a smart alec.'

'1955?'

'How do you know?'

'Everyone in this town knows that.'

'Well, now you know it too. That means you're part of it.'

I pull my coat more tightly around my shoulders. I don't think so.

I'm up my tree now. There's warm rain falling but the broad, flat leaves keep me dry enough. I can't actually see the river but I know it's there. First, there's the road and then it drops down to the market gardens all flat and brown with splashes of shiny green lettuces and other vegetables that I don't recognise. Then there's a line of trees. They straggle around like a line of kids and I know the river is there. We saw it in the first week. Dad took us for a drive, down across the river flats and over the old White Bridge and we looked down on the slow-moving, brown water. All the rivers are like that out here.

If there was another flood, *when* there's another flood, I can watch it from up here. I'll watch it and then I'll have something to tell.

At breakfast, Dad told me to shush, he wanted to listen to the weather report. I told him he wasn't a farmer so why did he bother. He said everyone should bother and why didn't I listen.

Over the crunching of my cereal, I heard them say it was also raining up north and the rivers were sending huge amounts of water down into New South Wales.

'In a few days,' said Dad, 'some of that water will reach us, and when it does, when it joins up with that river out there,' he pointed across the road, 'we could be in for something.'

'A flood?'

He shrugged.

The river is up. Wayne Drury said that when the school bus drove over the White Bridge this morning you could see the water without leaning out the window. He says they reckon it might break its banks tonight. When I asked if that meant a real flood Mr Burrows said no. He says the water will just wash over the river flats and it won't even get up to the road.

He's wrong. I'm on flood watch. I sit up in my tree and I stare out across the road and the flats. That water is going to come right up and over the market gardens, the road, the footpath and our front lawn. It'll be up to the verandah and into the house. And I will see it all.

It's broken its banks. It's up and onto the flats. They say that if it keeps raining, if the water from up north links up with it, if it

Rain • Libby Gleeson

comes much higher it might wash over the bridge and even cut the road. Then the town will be split in half.

Mr Burrows says they won't close the school; they'll just put all the kids on the train because the railway bridge is much higher and has never, ever been cut by the river. Kids on the farms far out are already cut off. Wayne and Amy didn't come in today. We aren't allowed out in the playground. It's full of puddles and the little kids put their gumboots on and splashed around in it seeing who could get the spray to go highest. So now we're all stuck inside.

From here, up my tree, I can see the water on the ground just this side of the line of trees. No-one thinks it'll spread right out. But it will. I know.

Mum's calling me to come in out of the rain. She reckons I'll catch a cold but the rain is warm and there's no wind. If I come down from my branch, if I stop watching the river, the rain might stop, the water might go down.

This morning, before Mum and Dad got up, I was out of bed. I put on the old waterproof pants that Mum wore to go skiing before I was born and I squelched across our soggy lawn. Then I was up my tree. The water was halfway across the river flats. There are pools and puddles all the way to the edge before the road. By the time I get back from school, they might all have joined up and there'll be just a sheet of water from the trees to the road. A giant lake. Then all we need is another two days of rain and it could be up and over the road and into our yard.

I can't wait.

Sandra Miller brought photos in today. They are from that great flood and her mum is just a little kid, in a boat going past the post office. Behind her you can see that the water is over the windows in the flower shop. Sean O'Leary said that that was his grandmother's shop and after the flood the business never really recovered and they had to sell up.

We have a worksheet about global warming and climate change. I'm watching the drops of water run down the window. Dad says some people bet on which drop will get to the bottom first. The rain is lighter now. I hope it doesn't stop.

When I got to my tree this afternoon I was sure the pools in the middle of the market garden were bigger. There's one that goes all the way from the tractor shed to the dirt path between the vegetable rows. And the path is nearly all under water. Will it fill up the whole garden and get to the road tonight?

It's there. I raced out when there was just enough light to see. A man was walking his dog along the road and I went across to join him and to look at the water lapping up to the grassy edges. Rain dripped from his eyebrows and ran down his cheeks.

'It's just like '55,' he said, and kept on walking.

I climbed up to my branch so quickly that I scraped my elbow and it bled but I didn't care. I'm not cold. I can see only water from the road to the trees. All the green vegetables and grapevines are gone. It's a lake, a sea. There are even tiny waves when the wind blows strongly and the rain is still falling. I am on a desert island with an ocean all around me.

I don't want to go to school today. I want to watch as the water creeps across the road and into our yard.

Dad says it won't. He says I have to go and that when I get back this afternoon it will be just where it is now. He says the water from the rivers up north won't be here for days.

He doesn't know what I know.

Everything is wet. The classroom smells wet. I want to say something about the water across the road from our place but

Rain ~ Libby Gleeson

Casey Saunders gets in first. She says that what we've had so far is nothing. She says that when the water went down from the last flood all the grass was dead and the smell was so bad that you always felt like spewing and you had to put a scarf over your face. There were dead animals too and it was ages and ages before they cleaned it all up.

The bridge is cut. The kids had to go home on the train. Some people couldn't go home from work and are staying with friends on this side of the river. There are bulletins about the roads every fifteen minutes on the radio and there's been a helicopter with a television film crew right over our house. They can't see me. The water's not draining off the road. Cars going past our place send spray high in the air. I can't see where the road ends and the dip down to the market garden begins.

Mum says that when there's a flood the snakes and other animals come out of the bush ahead of the water, but I haven't seen any yet.

It's all over the road. Cars still get through but slowly. We all listen to the weather report and Dad doesn't have to tell me to shush or anything. Mum says I have to go to school. I think they should close it. I could stay home and sit up here and watch as that water creeps across the lawn and up to our steps. I bet other kids' parents let them stay home — especially the ones with sheep and chooks and cows. When they get back to school they'll have so much to tell.

Mum thinks I'm in class. Instead I crept back by the lane that runs behind the fire station. I got wet but I don't care. I stuffed my bag in the back shed and took out my rain jacket with the hood so the drips don't go down my neck. I took some rope too and I've tied the branches back so there's a roof of leaves and none brushing against my face. The wind is behind me.

Rain · Libby Gleeson

It's a perfect spot. I've got my lunch and I'm going to stay up here. If I stop watching, it'll stop raining and then the water will go down.

That big wall of water is surging down from Queensland. When it reaches us there will be an almighty collision. BOOM. More water will surge up across the top of the bank and spread out over the flat. The rain will keep on falling and the water will race up over the road, then the footpath. It won't be long before it will be under our gate and into our yard. It will cover the flowers around the gate and along the path. From my branch I'll watch it lap around the steps, then up to the front door and then it will seep under the timber and into the house. Mum and Dad will be moving our stuff up on top of tables and wardrobes and they will call me to get ready because the boat is coming to take us to higher ground. But the boat won't come. Not yet. There are others in more danger than we are, people on lower ground so I will call to Mum and Dad to join me and they will wade through the water and climb up the tree to my branch. We will be the last ones to be rescued. We will be taken in our boat along the main street past all the shops where the water is washing against the windows and the awnings of the verandahs. We will pass the school where the water has seeped into every classroom and our books are floating through the open doorways. Branches of trees and leaves and bits of furniture will drift past us and I will reach down and pull into our boat a dog, struggling to swim in the murky waters. There'll be a storm with thunder and lightning and our boat will rock just like it's on the ocean but we'll all hold on tight and reach high ground safely. The whole town will be waiting and they will cheer us and clap us and all the kids will gather round to hear my story.

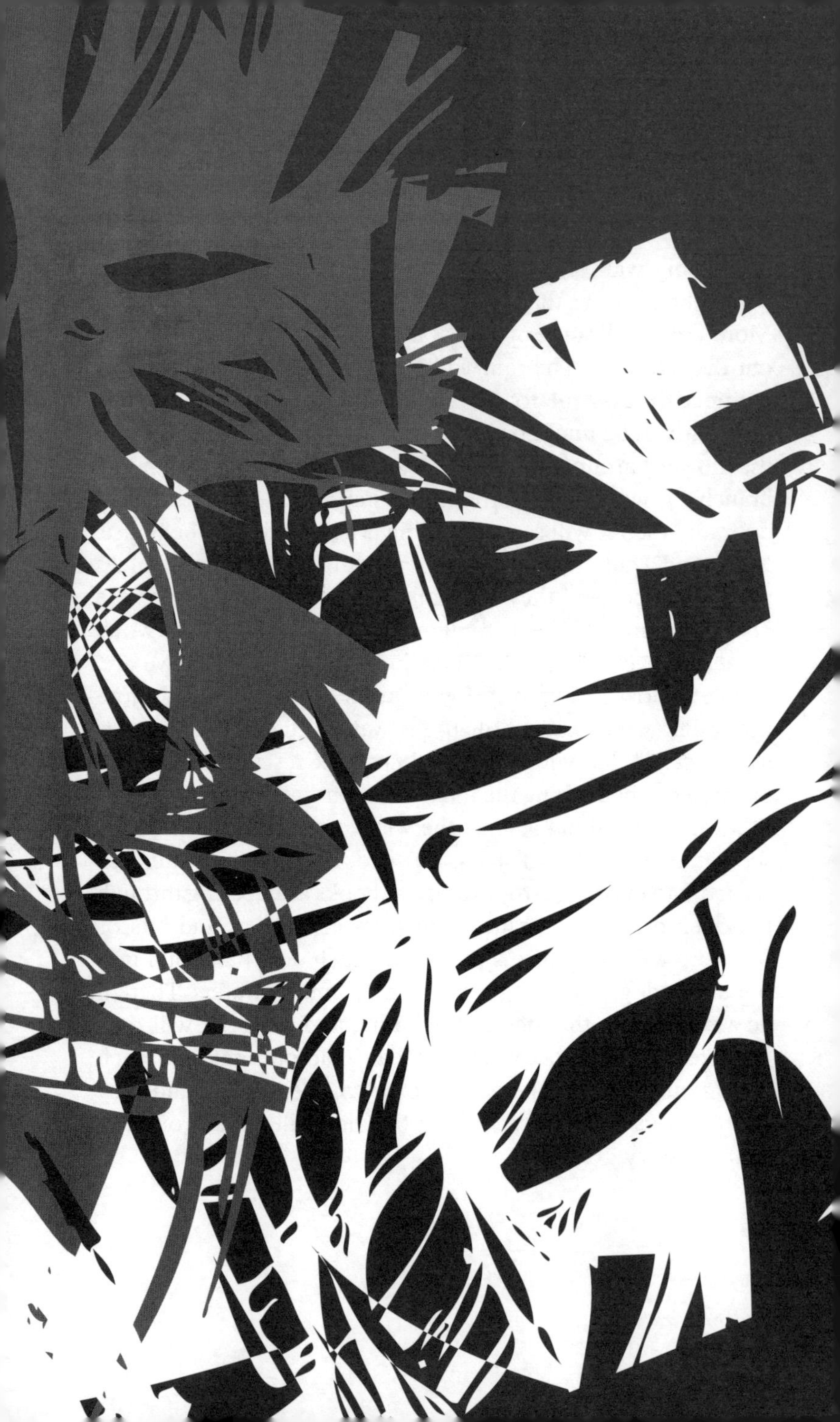

The Red Shoes

Isobelle Carmody

The Red Shoes · Isobelle Carmody

AMERIE was reading a book her mother had left her. On the flyleaf was written: *To my darling daughter, Amerie, on her birthday*. Amerie had found the book in the back of the bookshelf still wrapped and she was trying to understand what it could mean.

Andersen's Fairy Tales Revisited by Ander Pellori was inscribed across the front page in swirling important looking golden letters. And all around the golden letters, goblins and fairies and sprites cavorted and danced in a frenzied celebration.

Amerie could remember little of her mother whom her father said had left them both.

'She left us just before Amerie was five, and she broke our hearts,' her father said whenever anyone asked. And that was all he would say.

The first time she overheard her father say that, Amerie worried that she had not been treated for the heart that was broken when her mother left. She did not mention it to her father because his heart was wounded too. She felt a kind of deep ache whenever she thought of her mother, and imagined that there was a dribble of blood still leaking out of her heart. It seemed to her that talking and thinking of her mother reopened the wound, and so she did not speak for her father's sake. For he brooded darkly and rarely smiled.

Once she had heard him tell her teacher that she was too young to remember her mother, but that was not so. It was true that she did not remember her doing the sorts of things other girls' mothers did. She had no memory of her mother ironing or pushing a trolley in a supermarket or going to have her hair done. She had no memory of her mother stirring a pot, nor even of her dressed in a business suit and carrying a briefcase the way Raelene's mother did.

Amerie's memories were anything but ordinary.

The reason her father thought that she did not remember her mother was because she never spoke of her. That was partly to save him pain, but mostly because the memories were so strange she had kept them secret and silent inside her.

One of the memories was of both her parents arguing.

'I'm sick of this ...' her father had growled through his black beard.

Her mother had said in her soft cooing voice, 'Shh, Jon. You'll wake the baby.'

'If you were not so flighty ...'

'I do what I must do,' her mother had said in a pleading voice. 'You know that. When we married I warned you how it was with me and you said you understood.'

'I did not know it would take you away from me so often, or that you would consort with those creatures ...'

'You are jealous, and there is no need. I do not love my companions as men. They are like me and they understand how it is to be possessed by ...'

'Nothing and no one will possess you but me,' her father had said in his heavy voice. 'You belong to me.'

'I will not let you cage me ...'

There the memory broke off suddenly. The talk of flight and birds and cages had shivered Amerie's soul because of another memory. The most secret memory of all.

Her mother came to her wrapped in the shadows of the night, and stroked her face and kissed her as she lay drowsily in her bed.

'I will come back to you soon ...'

But her mother had not been entirely human in that memory. Woven through her dark lustrous hair were sleek black feathers, and Amerie's hand felt them on her breast and shoulder as well. As if she had not quite changed all the way into a bird yet.

There was only one other memory. Amerie's favourite. Her mother's hair was out of its usual bun and flowing all around her shoulders and Amerie was permitted to brush it. A black feather fluttered out onto the floor. The wind caught it up and tried to whisk it out of sight, but Amerie jumped down and ran lightly across the floor to catch it in her hand. Her mother laughed softly when she brought back her treasure. Looking around to be sure when they were alone, she closed Amerie's fingers around the feather and said, 'You are half me, little one, and one day you will fly. I see it in your movements. You are light as a feather.' Then for a moment she looked sad and proud all at once. 'You will long for the red shoes as I do and no price will be too high. You will fly because it is in your blood ...'

Amerie did not remember her mother going away. Nor even which order the memories had happened in. She had not understood all of the memories, but she had known from them that her mother *was not entirely human*. She was a thing of lightness and dark feathers, and music could move her to dance as the wind moves a feather. Part of her yearned to fly even when she was in human form. Amerie had often seen her dance and sway on her toes, flinging her arms out like wings. She did not look entirely human either. She was not round and soft and comfortable like the mothers of other girls. She was very thin and her legs and arms were bony and hard with muscles. *From flying*, Amerie knew now.

And Amerie was like her mother. Much as she ate, she was not heavy and solid like her father. She was slender and light-boned and her feet were narrow like her mother's though they lacked the queer calluses that must come to her in her bird form.

The Red Shoes — Isobelle Carmody

Once she had heard a neighbour tell her father after a visit that she ate like a bird.

But more than her body, she knew what she was because sometimes she would feel a strange yearning for something more than life could give. Something nameless and demanding and wonderful would dance through her blood, heady and intoxicating. Her fingers and feet would tingle and she would realise that she was on the verge of shapechanging, as her mother had done. But she was half her father as well, and she realised that the fleshiness of him weighed her down and caged her bird self, just as he had wanted to cage her mother.

Amerie had never been able to bear to see birds caged after she realised the truth. Outside pet shops, she would watch them, and they would look into her eyes and know she was part bird and understand her longing to free them. If no one were watching, she would slip open the catch and the birds would fly away.

Some did. Others just crouched against the bars in fear because they had been caged too long. Even shaking the cage would not make them fly because they had forgotten how.

That frightened Amerie because in those terrified birds she saw herself trapped forever. Too frightened to fly. She understood from this that if she did not learn to fly, there would be a day when the urge would leave her and she would come to accept the cage.

After this for a time she sought out and opened every cage she could find, hoping that if she could free enough birds, she would free her own birdself. Because she felt sure her mother had not left her willingly, but only for fear of her father's cage. She must pray for me to fly to her, Amerie knew, pray that her daughter would come to her birdself in time.

Oh, how she longed to fly away from her father's thick angry silences and his black thorny beard. His hand was hard and sometimes when he hugged her, she felt he was trying to make a cage of his body and put her inside it so that she would be trapped there forever beside his great red beating heart, fluttering and fluttering in despair.

In the end a pet-shop owner caught and shook her, asking if she did not understand that the birds were safe when they were caged; that other bigger birds and cats and all manner of predators would eat them now she had let them go, because the poor birds did not understand the danger of freedom.

'They are tame birds and tame birds must be caged!' the pet-shop man had said, giving her a final shake and warning her that if he saw her near his shop again he would call the police.

Walking away, shaken to her core, she understood that to accept the cage and to forget to fly was to be tamed. While to fly was dangerous freedom. Her mother had chosen to fly away because her father had wanted to tame her. He had wanted her to forget to fly and swoop and sing. He had wanted her safe in a cage, just as he wanted Amerie safe. He held her hand when they walked in the street in his big tight grip to keep her safe.

But to be safe, one had to be tamed, and being tamed meant you would never fly again.

And the predators? Amerie thought of them seriously, cats with flashing wicked eyes and who knew what other sinister beasts waiting to eat up freedom. But then another awareness came to her so powerfully that she stopped in the street and stared in front of her with fear and wonder, because she understood at last how her mother's sadness could have joy in it.

If it was in her to fly, she must fly! She *could not choose* to be tamed and safe in a cage because freedom was in her blood and would never permit it. Though she might die by the teeth or under the wheels of a car, she must fly. The urge was so strong that it was like a beast inside her, roaring to be free. She must

The Red Shoes • Isobelle Carmody

fly, else that inner beast would tear her to pieces with its own teeth. She would be alive, but she would be dead inside.

She tried not to open any more cages after that. Her father frightened her when he was angry and he would be very angry if he knew what she had done. All the more because he would know at once why she was releasing birds from their cages. If she gave the slightest hint that freedom raged through her veins, he would find some way to cage her. He must never know, and so she was careful to pretend she was tame.

Instead of dancing around the room or singing, which brought his heavy glowering gaze to press her down to the earth, she would sit quietly and read.

That seemed to please him and he would lay his great hand on her head and say that she was a good girl. He did not understand that while her body was still when she read, her mind flew far and wide. She would only dance and swirl and let her bird spirit move her body to music when her father went out to church on Sunday evenings. That was the only time he left her alone. Only then, as she dipped and leapt, did she dare to pray to her mother to help her learn to fly before it was too late.

And now, the book. Her mother must have flown back in secret to hide it, knowing that searching for books on her own shelf in her father's library, she would find it. Her eighth birthday was only a few days away. Amerie held the book tightly against her chest, understanding that she had been given a warning. If she did not fly before her eighth birthday, she would be too heavy and the urge to freedom would be tamed.

Her heart pounded against her chest, the mended crack aching with the force of it, as she opened the precious gift.

The hair on her neck stiffened because the first story was called 'The Red Shoes'.

The Red Shoes • Isobelle Carmody

Shivering with excitement, Amerie began to read.

It was the story of a girl who longed for a pair of red dancing shoes so desperately, she forgot to care for her dying grandmother. She dreamed of nothing but the red shoes and eventually stole money to buy them. But when she put them on, they danced her until she was exhausted. They would not be removed for they had grown to her feet. They danced her into a ragged urchin, and finally a woodcutter offered to chop them off her. 'So that you may be still and quiet at last.' The girl was frightened because it meant he must chop off her feet as well, and she would not ever dance again. 'I will carve wooden feet and strap them to your legs so that you can hobble around. You will never dance again, it is true, but look where dancing has brought you. Let me chop off your feet and you will be safe.'

And the girl had bowed her head and wept as she agreed.

Amerie closed the book, frightened by what she had read. Her mother had once told her she would fly when she wore the red shoes, but here was a story of magical shoes that would not be removed unless your feet were chopped off as well. Her mother's message must be riddled into the story, and she would have to fathom it.

That night, she slept with the book under her pillow. She lay awake for a long time, thinking of all the magical shoes she had encountered in stories. Puss-in-boots had boots that carried him seven leagues at a single step, and that was a kind of flying. And Cinderella had been given glass slippers by her Fairy Godmother, and in them she had flown to the heart of her prince. Then there were the red shoes Dorothy had got from the Wicked Witch of the West, which took her anywhere she wanted if she clicked the heels together …

When Amerie slept, it was to dream that she was the girl wearing the red dancing shoes, whirling and dancing and leaping herself to exhaustion, and yet, though she was half

The Red Shoes ♣ Isobelle Carmody

dead, her heart laughed and danced inside her and freedom flowed through her soul like a river.

The woodcutter came to her big as a bear in the moonlight. He had a black beard and a red mouth, and he carried a silver axe with two cruelly sharpened edges.

'I will make sure you don't fly away. I love you and I will tame you.'

Amerie was frightened, but the delight in her blood ate up the fear and she danced in a circle around the great heavy woodcutter. 'I will not let you cage me.'

The woodcutter made a lunge for her, but she danced out of his grasp and ran until she came to her own house in the middle of the dark woods. Somewhere a wolf howled as she threw open the door and ran up the stairs. She could hear her father's feet on the veranda. The front door slammed open.

'Come to me,' his voice boomed. 'Let me cut off the red shoes and you will be safe.'

Higher, the shoes whispered.

But there was no higher. Except …

Amerie turned to look at the attic stairs. Her father had forbidden her to climb them. The roof is dangerous and unstable and you will fall through it, he had said.

Higher, the shoes whispered urgently.

She ran up the wooden steps, light as a bird on the snow. Up and up and into the roof. It was dark and the roof slanted deeply. Moonlight streaming in through the dormer window lit up boxes and cases and heaps of clothing; it silvered a lace of tulle and a dressmaker's dummy festooned with spider webs.

'I know you are up there. I will kill you before I will let you leave me again …' cried her father, and now his feet were thunder on the stairs. 'If I cannot have you, no one will have you.'

The Red Shoes • Isobelle Carmody

Higher, whispered the red shoes.

There is no higher, Amerie thought.

Then you will be tamed and you will die ... the red shoes whispered.

'I love you!' roared her father, his boots clumping on the wooden attic steps, shaking the house.

❧

Amerie woke up.

Her face and hands were slick with sweat as she reached under the pillow and took out the book. The cover was cool and velvety as a puppy's belly under her hot hands, and she lay there until the sun rose, holding the book tightly to her, trying to think what to do. She must get up into the attic and find the red shoes that would show her how to fly. But her father would not leave her alone until Sunday and that would be her eighth birthday and it would be too late. She would be trapped forever.

She must get into the attic, but her father had forbidden it. She must get him to leave her alone. But how?

'Are you all right?' her father rumbled that evening. She had sat very quietly all day, not even reading.

'I feel sick,' Amerie said in her palest voice.

Her father's black brows pulled together over his dark eyes and he took her chin in his big hand and lifted it so that he could look into her eyes. Amerie prayed he would not smell the talc on her cheeks.

'You look sickly, my little one. Perhaps I should bring you to the doctor tomorrow.'

Amerie's heart thumped. 'Maybe if you give me some of the tonic you gave me last time, I will be better by morning.'

He frowned again, then shrugged. 'We will try it.'

He went to the bathroom, but the bottle was empty.

The Red Shoes — Isobelle Carmody

'That is strange. The bottle is finished. I will go and buy some more. You had better get into your bed.'

She gave him a docile nod, and went up to her bedroom. A moment later, she heard the front door close. She ran to the attic steps and hurried up them, and just as in the dream, there were boxes and a dressmaker's dummy with her mother's slender shape, and in the corner near the dormer window, a froth of gauzy tulle.

But no red shoes.

Her father would only be away a little while and she must find them and return to her bed before he came back. Frantically, she began to search. Under clothes and dresses and a suitcase of silky woman's clothing. There were lots of shoes but none were red. She opened the top of one of the boxes and found letters.

One began, 'My dearest Winter, Jonathon must understand that you need to dance, surely. Did he not first see you soaring on the stage? Does he think you can just stop as if you were a secretary typing letters?'

Winter was her mother's name, Amerie knew, setting the letter aside. She had obviously left all of her letters and clothing behind because in her bird form she had no need for them. Her father had told people she had gone away because he wanted no one to know he had married a shapechanger.

But where were the red shoes? Surely that was what the dream had meant. She opened another box and another. She had no idea how much time had passed, but she had not heard her father's tread on the steps yet, and so she decided to take a few more moments to search.

Help me, Mother ... she whispered.

Her eyes fell on the silvery tulle, and she noticed a black feather caught in it. Her heart leapt.

Then she heard her father's boots on the wooden veranda.

The Red Shoes • Isobelle Carmody

She pulled at the tulle; there was masses of it. It was a kind of dress, and though white and silver, the bottom of the hem was thick with darkness, and there were black and white feathers stuck there. And there, under the tulle were dark slender dancing shoes with long silky tapes. They looked black, but the moon made red look black, she reminded herself. Without thinking, she pushed her feet into them. There was a crackle and a roughness inside, as if someone had put red paint in the shoes as well as on the outside, but they fit her perfectly in the heel. They are too long, but I will grow into them, she thought dreamily.

'Amerie?'

Her father was on the second floor and it was too late now to go down and get into her bed because he would see her. She listened to him going into her bedroom as she tied the tapes round and round, making a neat bow at the rear.

'Amerie. Are you up there?' her father growled. He was at the bottom of the attic steps.

She stood up, thinking she must hide. Perhaps, then, he would think she had gone out and go looking for her. And she would come down and pretend she had ...

His boots clumped purposefully on the steps.

'Amerie, I know you're up there. I told you never to go up there. I warned you and you would not listen. You are just like your mother ...'

Amerie heard an axe in his voice and was frightened, but the red shoes filled her with joy. *I must hide*, she thought.

He will find you, whispered the shoes.

Amerie thought of the dream and whirled to the dormer window. It was open and she could fit through. Outside the moon shone like a bowl of silver water.

Higher or you will die ...

The Red Shoes • Isobelle Carmody

Amerie understood then, and she hesitated and looked down at the shoes. They looked black, but surely they were the red shoes. In this darkness she could not tell. But she felt them growing onto her, filling her with feathers and the urge to fly. She looked down at the book her mother had sent as a message. The gold lettering was silver now and winked at her as if to say she must choose now and forever.

And she laughed. *I cannot choose, for I must fly, it is in me ...*

And she flew.

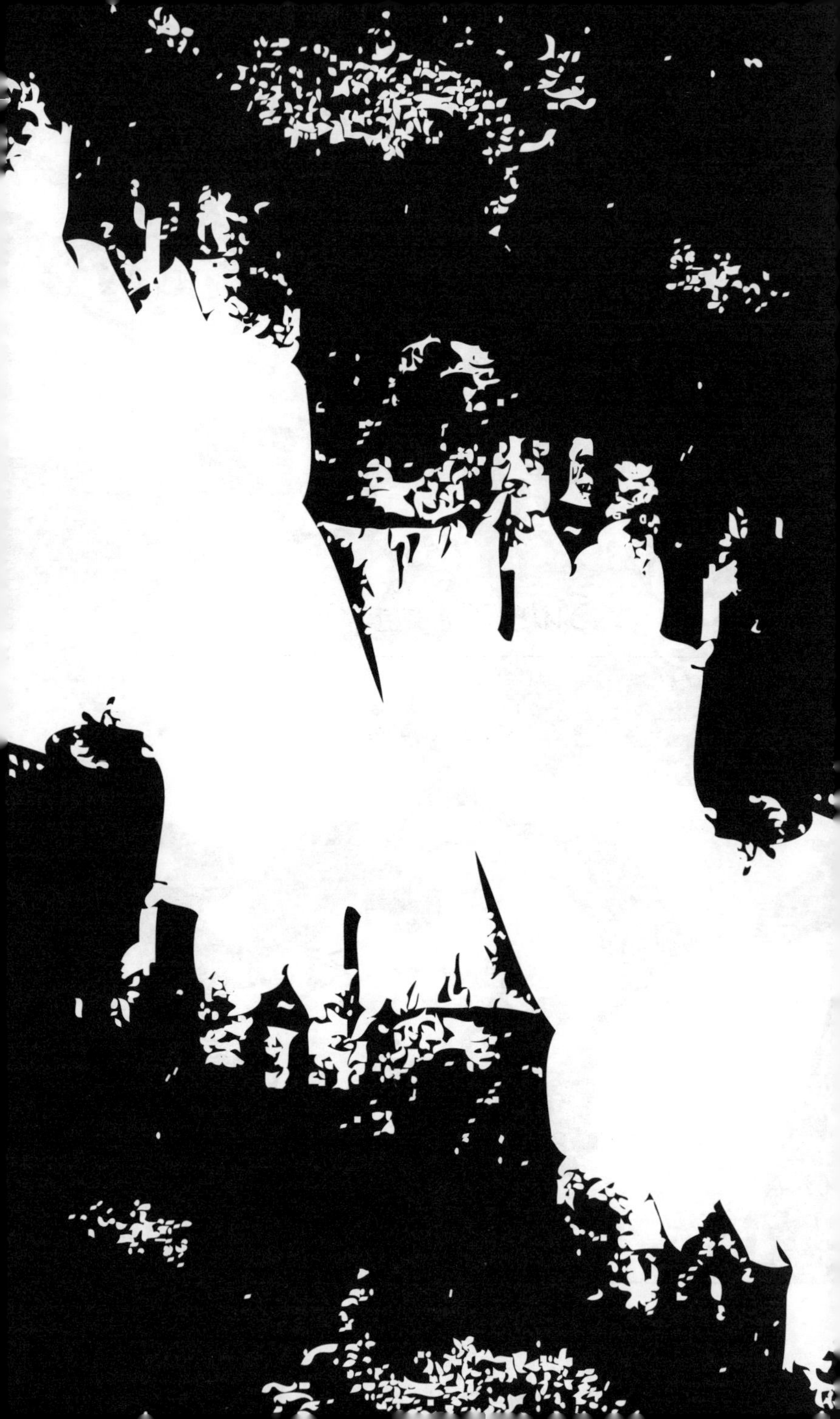

SWEET PIPPIT

Margo Lanagan

Sweet Pippit ❧ Margo Lanagan

WE SET out in the depth of night, having held ourselves still all evening. Hloorobnool was poor at stillness, being only in her fifties. But our minder was a new man; he likely thought she rocked and puffed and raised her trunk like that every sunset. We could all have reared up and trumpeted, no doubt, without alarming that one. But our suffering was close to the surface; better to keep it packed into a tight circle than to risk rampage and shooting by letting it show.

With the man gone to his rest, Booroondoonhooroboom set to work. She used her broken tusk on the gateposts, on the weak places where the hinges had been reset after Gorrlubnu's madness. Pieces pattered to the ground as softly as impala dung. She worked and she sang, drawing the lullaby up around us. Before long we were all swaying in our night-stances, watching Booroondoon with our ears and our foreheads as well as our eyes.

And then she had done loosening.

'Gooroloomboon,' she said, and Gooroloom came forward. The two of them lifted aside the chained-together gates, and there between the gateposts was a marvellous wide space. We had not expected it, somehow—though had we not all said, and planned, and agreed? Ah, it is a difficult thing, the new, and none of us like it much. We swayed and regarded the open gate. We were accustomed at the most to circling these gardens, with an owda on our back full of tickling peeple, and our mahout on our head.

It took Booroondoon, our queen and mother, still singing very low, to move into the space, to show us that bodies such as ours *could* move from home into the dark beyond. And as soon

Sweet Pippit · Margo Lanagan

as the darkness threatened to take her, to curtain her from our sight, it became not possible for any of us to stay.

And so we moved, unweighted, from the gardens; Hmoorolubnu took my tail, as if that small thing would hold her steady in this storm of freedom. Zebu groaned at us behind their rails, and a goat on the stone hill lifted its head and gave brittle cry. But our bearing is the sort that soothes others; we move with inevitability, as the stars do, as the moon swells and shrinks upon the sky. We brushed aside the wooden gate-house as if it were a plaything we had tired of, and the other animals remained calm. Gooroloom tumbled it to sticks, and our feet crushed it to dust. Above the dark and swollen river of our rage, my delight in our badness hung briefly bright.

His name was something like Pippit. It was too short for our ears to catch, as all peeple's names are; twig-snaps and bird-cheeps, they finish before they properly start. But his smell was a lasting thing, and his hand. Pippit of all peeple could tell badness from goodness, as we could. He would know that this was our only choice, he who could still us with a word, whose slender murmuring soothed us when all other voices were pitched too high and madding, who slept fearless among our feet and rode us without spear or switch—whom we missed in a rage of missing, ever since he had been taken from us to somewhere in the dark out-world.

Gooroloomboon spoke through her forehead, wonderingly: 'How our minds have become circle-shaped, from all our circling, squared from pacing that square! Once we were wild! But I fear I have no wildness any more, Booroondoon; maybe wildness has died in my blood and my feet can move *only* in circle and square. What are we to do for water and for food, mother? And how are we to know where to find our sweet Pippit? And if he be in a place that requires badness to reach him, can we do such a thing, even in his name?'

Booroondoon, her graciousness, heard Gooroloom out. 'Put away your fears,' she said, even as she lullabied. 'Fears are for little-hearts, or the lion-hunted. I have never been wild in my life, yet our Pippit's track through this world is as clear as a stripe of water thrown across a dry riverbank. What you love this much, you can always find again.'

And our spirits, which had been poised to sink with Gooroloom's worry, lifted as if Booroondoon's words were buoyant water, as if her songs were breeze and we were wafted feathers.

We walked out among peeple's houses, that were like friends standing beside the path. With every sleeping house we passed, I was more wakeful; with every step I took that was not circle-path, or earth we had trodden as many times as there are stars, something else broke open in me. My mind seemed a great wonderland, largely unexplored, my body a vast possibility of movements, in any directions, all new. There would be food and water, good and bad—Gooroloom would smell them, too, when she finished fretting. I wanted to lift my head and trumpet, but there was joy also in knowing I must not, in moving with my fellows through the sleeping town, making no sound but planting feet and rubbing skin and the breath of walking free.

We came to the town's edge. Without pausing, Booroondoon continued on under the moon towards nothing, only parasol trees that cannot be eaten, only a line that had stars above it, dry shadows below. We followed, and the town smells fell behind. Hloorobn, ahead of me, lifted her trunk. I head-bunted her rump, to keep her quiet, and she grunted low in surprise. Then we settled to a strong pace after Booroondoon, rolling our yearning rage out onto the plain.

Several hours on, we were suddenly among the bones. Heightened as our senses were, we'd not anticipated these. And it is always difficult to move on from such places. Hloorobn, in particular, hung by the remains of her mother, our sister,

Gorrlubnu, lifting and turning the bones, urging us to take and turn them also, tipping the great headbone with a thud and a puff of moon-silvered dust.

Booroondoon went among the bones telling the names once only, touching the heads and leaving us to turn the lesser bones. Then she waited beyond, facing our goal but in all other respects patient, allowing us our youth and rawness and powerful pain, though her own was long ago distilled into wisdom and grace.

We went on, our thoughts like weighted owdas slowing our steps.

We walked far that night. Booroondoon said we should go straight out, for an improbable distance that peeple would not follow.

'And if they do?' said jittery Hloorobn. 'If they surprise us?'

'What can they do against so many Large?' said Booroondoon. 'Cannot herd if we will not listen. Can try, with their spear, but will have to spear us all to stop us.'

She meant that such a spearing was not likely. But then, their taking Pippit had not been likely, either, yet it happened. In this night of walking in the wild, nothing was certain as it used to be.

Towards dawn, we found water. There was no town behind us, no town ahead, only grassed plain, and rounded rocks like friends browsing. When we had drunk, we moved straight on, slower for a while to try the wild grass, pulled up sweet and still living. Booroondoon sang no longer, for we did not need to be led by that means now; we had seen our own courage and were rallied and moved and unstoppable.

So the day passed, and several others like it. There was a night and day of terrible thirst, born of the need to walk a straight line from our starting point. Then we came to a broad, clear river, and we swam it, and stood in the shallows on the far side, and the water was magnificent in our throats, a delight across our backs.

Late that day, when we had satisfied our thirst and settled the fears arising from it, Booroondoon said, 'The place we want is not far now.'

We sensed it, a big, rubbishy restlessness far down-river, a swarming movement in the ground that made our feet unhappy.

'We must go into the midst of that?' said Gooroloom.

'They will not bring him out to us,' said our wise mother.

We walked awhile on the thought.

Then, 'I have it,' said Booroondoon. 'We will walk into the town as if we were led, so as to calm the little-hearts. We will go in a line, trunk to tail, and with care where the way is narrow. We must move slowly, for our Pippit's smell may be easily lost among all the others, markets and meateries and skinworks and the like. But if we go graciously and let neither dogs nor peeple fright us—do you hear me, Hloorobn?—if we stay together in our line, we cannot be thwarted.'

'As you say, mother and queen,' we replied.

We decided we would go into the town just before day hurried out of night, when the smells and peeple-movements would be less. Until that hour we lurked at a distance, in a bad place—stenchful, with death-birds crowding sky and ground.

Their headwoman flapped to the top of the rubbish nearest us. 'Any of youse sick?' she skrarkled, eyeing us all.

Hloorobn rumbled too low for her to hear.

'Anyone dropping a baby soon? Youse all look pretty big,' said the bird hopefully.

Booroondoon swung up her trunk, and the bird staggered away: 'Just asking, just asking!'

'Disgusting,' said Hloorobn.

Sweet Pippit :▲ Margo Lanagan

'Shudderable,' Gooroloom agreed.

'Take no notice,' said Booroondoon. 'We are Larger.'

There was nothing to eat in this place, so we began, in the night, to feel wretched, all bulk and no bone, our minds spinning like the moon on its wheel.

'If only he were here,' said Gooroloom, 'if only we already had him! This venture frightens me, now it is near to finishing.'

It was good that she spoke, or my own fears would have bubbled up into my forehead and made themselves known. I could not keep Gorrlubnu out of my head, how after months of uncanny stillness, where Pippit soothed and Booroondoon leant and all of us huddled around her, she had slipped her mind as your foot slips a loose tether-loop, and gone crashing from our lives; how she burst the gates with her head and bent them underfoot; how, unthinkably, she left Booroondoon's commands ignored upon the air. We stood voiceless and mindless, as peeple leaped and twinkled after her. At Booroondoon's knee, tiny Pippit jolted as Gorrlubnu struck about her; he cried out when she roared. She swam away through the market. Fruits sagged out of their pyramids and broke on the ground; chicken cages tumbled and sprayed feathers.

The marketers came to the gate-opening, yabbering and shaking their fists at Pippit, but we had ears only for the receding commotion of our sister, Gorrlubnu, the drumbeat of her madness, and the lesser impacts and explosions around it. Until a single blunderbuss shot saved her from worse rampage, bringing all other sounds to stillness, so that across the town, through all its wreckage and outrage, we heard clearly the thunder-crash that was Gorrlubnu striking the ground; her lips shuddering on the breath thus crushed from her; the dry scrape of her feet dying in the dust.

She has found the Forest Hills of legend, breathed Booroondoonhooroboom, our queen. *She is pressing her forehead against the first browsing-tree.*

Sweet Pippit • Margo Lanagan

Only singing brought us through that hungry night amongst the refuse, a tether of rumbling song through the slowest part of the sun's race round. Whenever my thoughts made me fall quiet, the singing strengthened into my hearing, and drew me in again.

'Very well,' said Booroondoon in the deepest hour. We all heard her; none of us were asleep.

We walked a nightmare road. The cold breeze blew peeple-rubbish and rattled rotten paper. Would we lose our nose for Pippit, amongst all this ordure? Booroondoon moved ever queenly ahead.

The town began gradually, with rubbish-pickers' shelters, the children sleeping as if thrown down, bare on the bare ground. Then wood-walled houses sidled up to the road, which widened and hardened, and finally, along the cleanest avenues, brick and stone palaces rose higher than ourselves, textured with carvings. And after days of golden grass, and trees nearly black in their thirst, here were green vines and hanging plants spilling over the palace walls, their flowers set like jewels among their bright, water-fat leaves.

We came to a circle that seemed purpose-made for owda rides, within a ring of empty stalls. There we joined trunk to tail and became still, to listen and breathe, to arrive at the knowledge we needed.

And there Booroondoon said to us, at her lowest, at her farthest from peeple's hearing, 'He is close, very close.' She listened further, then spoke softer, no more than a gentle buzzing in our heads. 'And in sore distress.'

We took pains not to give voice, but anyone who knew us would have heard the trouble in our breathing, the creak of the strong will restraining our movement. Our rage squirmed and whimpered like a creature pinned underfoot, that must be kept from flight, but not be harmed.

Sweet Pippit ❧ Margo Lanagan

'We could break down the place,' rumbled Hloorobn.

'Hush!' we said.

'It would crush Pippit within,' Gooroloom remonstrated.

'We could tear off the doors,' Hloorobn whispered.

'But remember those peeple that took him,' I said, 'with their bright spears. How quick to anger they were! He had real fear of them, so we should, too.'

'There is a terrible smell on him,' said Booroondoon. She tilted her head a certain way, and some of us dropped tail from trunk, and Hloorobn even shifted one foot that way, for the smell was among us for a moment, a flash of fear-sweat, a shaft of some worse thing.

'We know that smell,' said Hmoorolubnu. Booroondoon grunted and twitched her head. All around, trunk rasped on flank, seeking and giving help. 'Our sister Gorrlubnu, remember?'

'No one has forgotten Gorrlubnu,' I hissed, from one of those moments when my tusks gleamed before my eyes, and my whole self seemed funnelled into them.

Others were at my side, leaning.

'Do you mean Pippit is mad?' asked Gooroloom of the queen, and lifted her trunk and sniffed carefully.

'Is dying,' said Booroondoon. 'Is moving towards death, sure as winter follows summer.'

'He is ill? He is beaten?' I said out of the deep woe that was like mud grasping us, sinking us down to death ourselves. I could not breathe to draw in the scent of him, my trouble was so great.

'Neither of those. He seems whole in body and strength. Only, that smell—' And again it was there, making me want to rear and run. 'I cannot puzzle it.'

'Can we find him?' I said in quiet agony. 'Is it safe to seek him?'

'Let us go and see,' said Booroondoon. She must have known we were about to break bond and rush in all directions. She knew well that it is better to give a little, early on, than to lose all at the last.

We took our places and went in line through trade streets that smelled of paint and spices, shaved metal and wood. Booroondoon brought us among palaces, grimed and weary-feeling. Low in a brick wall there, she found a hole, barred like the one in our night-house. From this one poured the cold stinks of fear, some of them stale when our mothers' mothers were birthed, and some fresh as just-pulled plains-grass, full of juice and colour.

Among them was Pippit's fear—even I could smell it. 'Little man, little man!' I heard myself croon, 'Day's light, night's peace, to what have they brought you?' And we were all around the barred hole, our feet puddling in the fears, and we all spoke, mostly only in our heads, but some in our throats where peeple might hear us, danger or no, we were so pained and grieved.

Then, wonder of wonders, from within the hole came a tiny voice that we knew, calling our names, those chips of bird-cheep he gave us. And we could not help but answer, in our woe.

Gooroloom fluttered a breath into the hole, and there was an immediate ruckus of many peeple in there. Hloorobn grasped one of the window-bars and plucked it out like a twig, and all the peeple inside went silent. She plucked out the other bars, laying them neatly as she had once laid cut logs in her forest work.

And as she pulled the last, peeple boiled out like ants, terrified peeple climbing over Goorooloom's trunk, crawling among our legs, smelling all of filth and illness, but none of them was Pippit. And when they had finished boiling, still Pippit was weeping and calling us from within.

Sweet Pippit ❧ Margo Lanagan

'What is it?' said Hloorobn. 'Have they broken some part of him?'

We drew in our breath at the thought.

'I told you, he is whole,' said Booroondoon. 'But he is deep inside this place. Perhaps there are more bars, between us and him; perhaps he is behind a gate too strong for peeple to breach.'

'But *we* could breach it—'

'Try, Hloorobn!' I urged. 'Get down on your knees and reach in!'

She did so, while we all whispered help and surance, past her head, to Pippit inside.

'There is nothing,' Hloorobn rumbled in disgust. 'Nothing but roof and air as far as I can reach. And there is no light. I can hear no chain—can you?—but their leg-tether may be of rope.'

'Do peeple leg-tether *each other*?' I asked astounded.

'What else would keep him from us? Listen to him, poor nubbet—if he could be with us, he would.' And indeed, I was fighting to listen to Hloorobn and not let my heart be stretched to breaking by the sound of Pippit's weeping.

We murmured to him, and he called to us, until we were all nearly mad with not seeing him, with not taking him up and placing him as a crown on our heads, with not feeling the pat of his little paws on our faces, or the trill of his song, almost too high for us to hear, as he plied the soapy hardbroom on all our backs in turn. What joy we had had, commanded by a Pippit, who knew no fear of us but only love, who cared for us so closely and so well—it was hard to remember that he was not a Large like one of us, and could not hear our loving head-talk.

'We must go,' wept Booroondoon at last. 'Dawn rushes towards us. We cannot reach him, and it will do him no good to hear us being speared out here.'

'They would never,' said Gooroloom. 'They only spear mad ones, like Gorrl—'

'We must go. Somewhere we can think, where we are not flayed by our beloved's sadness. If we stay here, we will fall to mindlessness with our pain, and do him no good.'

And so, suffering and weeping, we drew away.

'Will he know we intend to come back?' worried Hloorobn.

'The child is so close to death, we are no more than a dream to him,' soothed Gooroloom.

'And perhaps we can be no more than that comforting dream,' said Booroondoon. 'Perhaps we must be content with that.'

By some route I did not see, through a daze of mourning, Booroondoon led us to a cleared part of town. The smell of dead ashes lingered in the place, so a fire must have brought the structures down, but now all the rubble was gone, and the soil beneath was combed flat.

We tried to gather ourselves, but could do little more than sweep our woe back and forth. Was our only choice to turn and follow our own tracks home, and live out our long lives under fearful spike-men, stung by their beatings, nagged by their needling voices?

'I would rather seek the Forest Hills,' said Gooroloom. 'What is a life without Pippit?' And we mourned and sighed around her.

'Come, we must put our minds to this,' said Booroondoon. 'We must stand in a line as if we were peeple-bid, and let schemes brew in our heads.'

But no sooner had we arranged ourselves than the town began to stir around us.

'What is this?' said Hloorobn. 'Peeple never rise so early.'

'Not in such numbers,' said Gooroloom. 'Only marketers and street-sweepers come out before dawn.'

Sweet Pippit ॰ Margo Lanagan

'I do not like the feeling of it,' said Booroondoon.

As soon as she said it, my bones felt a deep unease, as if they could slip unset somehow, as if we might fall to pieces inside our skins. 'Nor I,' I whispered.

Even before the first few muffled peeple passed us, all walking the same way, we could feel that the town's quiet activity was bent like spring grass under a steady wind, an eagerness like river-water pulling. But instead of the sweetness of water, instead of the scents of bud and pollen and new leaf, this pulling breeze carried a low stink, a tang of chain-metal, a sour-sweet dreadfulness.

We stood close together as dawn came on, trying to find some other scent on the air to disperse the stink. 'I wish we were home again,' whispered Hloorobn. 'Around this time, he would be stirring away in the straw, our little man ... Do you remember when he first saw us, how the child ran to Booroondoon and flung his tiny arms about her leg?'

'We must go,' said Booroondoon, 'for he sleeps not on straw but on stone, and someone is kicking him awake even as we try for courage among our memories.' And she took a step after the passing peeple.

We joined on behind her, some silent, some wittering ('To that death-place?' 'Oh please, my queen!'). We moved after her, deeply against our will, in our orderly line, through the main town. The peeple in flood around us were too intent upon the dreadfulness to realise we went uncommanded. They flowed past full of fear and excitement and relief, their faces always towards their destination.

The place was crowded, with an itch in the air; it was the stuff of bad dreams, to have to pick one's way among such close-packed flimsies. But the platform at the centre, sweet with fresh-sawn wood, was empty, except for two men holding rattle-guns, which smelt not of death but of pride and show. What

Sweet Pippit ▸ Margo Lanagan

stank was the blade lying like a moon-sliver on the dark, raised box before them. Through all the crowd there was a craning and a yearning towards this weapon.

Peeple had brought food baskets, seating, children. As day brightened further, parasols began to open and twirl throughout the crowd. A man close by was selling burnt-sugar. One boy carried a small white rat on his shoulder.

'What breed of wrong-hearted festival is this?' I asked it.

'I don't know, but the food is good.'

The crowd was such that we could only form a line, Booroondoon by the platform and the rest of us sheltering behind her from the full force of the blade's stink. She rumbled a message: *Hold Hloorobn*, and I renewed my grasp on Hloorobn's tail. We were trained to be serene among peeple; their chatter stirred habitual serenity from our bones. But they were not our peeple, and this was not our town, and we were hungry and thirsty and afraid.

A macao-bird shrieked from the far side of the square: 'Here comes the fun-man, to start off the fun!'

Up the wooden steps climbed a much-bedizened person, with a head-plume, and sparkles on his shoulders. He stood tall between the two guards and spread his arms. The crowd quieted, and the plume-man spoke, his high voice carrying to all corners and every crowded balcony of the square. As he spoke, the peeple grew quieter, and their tides of feeling changed from puzzlement, to disappointment, and finally to alarm and unsettlement.

The macao gave an idiot laugh. 'No whippings today, folk! The monkeys have got out of their cage! The monkeys are running all over town, teasing the watchdogs and busting out the pantries!' Peeple began to pack away belongings, and to edge away from the platform through the crowd. The plume-man made a staying motion with his hands, and kept on speaking,

Sweet Pippit ~ Margo Lanagan

but peeple leaked away, until there were perhaps only half their number remaining. Now we could all move up alongside Booroondoon, and Gooroloom and I could press the excitable Hloorobn between us, flank to flank, and hold her steady.

'Here comes the chopper!' shrieked the macao with glee. 'And the choppee! Say goodbye to your head, bad monkey!'

'There,' said Booroondoon. 'At the great door.'

Raising my head above Hloorobn's I saw a little one, all filthy, being stumbled towards us by two men, also in the sparkling uniforms. Peeple spat on him and squeaked at him as he came. An eddy of breeze brought us his dirt and distress, his being undone by fear, but beneath all that, the familiar, fresh-straw smell of our mahout.

They pushed him up onto the wooden place; they thrust him to his knees there. And someone else had arrived. His close-suit, entirely blue-black, was like a slice of starless night. It covered his face, and stank. Peeple always move too quickly, but this happened in the taking of a single breath. No sooner had we seen him than the blue-black man was making the light flash from the blade, into all parts of the crowd. We were a row of confusions, locked in our mass, as self-less as boulders of the plain.

Then our little ragged one, our Pippit, lifted his head. His hair like dirty ribbons fell back from his face, and he saw us through his staring tear-filled eyes, and knew us.

His knowledge clanked closed upon us like the most welcome leg-iron. His mouth moved on the beloved sound of his command. All of us—in a vast sudden relief at having someone to obey, after our weeks of being chivvied by frightened peeple with sticks, after our days of wandering in the wilderness—all of us lowered our haunches and hoisted our heads and forelegs, to stand giant, to show our true height.

Sweet Pippit · Margo Lanagan

The peeple cleared around us like dust from a sharp blow of breath. Pippit commanded again, and I spoke back as he told me, as did my sisters and our mother our queen. The peeple ran farther away. We spoke with our entire hearts and our full bulk, and every arch and column shook with the noise.

Pippit's voice singled out Booroondoon. The rest of us stood giant, proclaiming our hugeness, trumpeting our obedience and our love.

Their eyes were all in a row, says Booroondoon now, *like children peeping over our garden wall, the men's who held him. The blade-man, he saw me coming; he knew what Pippit was commanding. It happened all so fast—he lifted his sword—he leaped, he was upon Pippit!—and what could I do?*

Nothing but what you did, we reassure her—although, when we saw her fling that blue-black rag out among the peeple, we knew it was a terrible thing she had been driven to.

And then I could just push the others away. Them I did not injure, those ones, did I? They stepped back quietly; they had no swords, you see, and they had seen what I did to the first—so in hurting one I saved at least two—

Also, you had him—

'I have him!' she rumbled to us, and Pippit called us in his bird-voice, even as she swung him onto her head. We moved towards our accustomed order. But seeing Pippit so small and unprotected at our head, and knowing the peeple wished him dead, I pushed forward to precede Booroondoon, as I would have for no other reason, and others came up to shelter him from peeple who might leap up from the sides. Out of the square we went, while the peeple foamed and cried and parted to let us through, and fell back farther as we left the paved part of the town, as we left the housed part, until there were only a few wide-eyed rubbish-pickers' tinies by the road to watch us pass,

Sweet Pippit ✤ Margo Lanagan

with our prize on our head, our live, sweet Pippit, chattering and laughing and greeting us by our bird-names over and over.

❦

Which is how we come to be here, on this long walk away from all we know. Since we left the road and the land began undulating, 'Our Pippit may be leading us to the Forest Hills of legend,' Hloorobn says eagerly.

Booroondoon in her sadder moments says, 'He may indeed be leading us into death, for I have never been this way before.'

'And you have been near everywhere there is to be, our queen,' says Gooroloom, 'from the log-camp mountains, to the ports, to the road-making settlements all up and down.'

Says Booroondoon, 'Yet I know nothing of this place, not its rocks or its creatures, nor how Pippit chooses the way among ten hundred sandhills all the same.'

'Who knows? Who minds?' says Hloorobn happily.

'None of us, that's sure,' says Gooroloom.

And none of us does. For each evening our sweet Pippit brings us to water and good browsing, and each morning we wake to a spray of his hot little voice, to the blessing of his kisses and his touch as he walks among us. And he lifts us without spike and leads us without wrath. Singing, always singing, he moves us onward, into each brightening day.